W. T. Harris

WILLIAM TORREY HARRIS
1835 -- 1935

WILLIAM TORREY HARRIS

1835 -- 1935

A Collection of Essays, including Papers and Addresses presented in Commemoration of Dr. Harris' Centennial at the St. Louis Meeting of the Western Division of the American Philosophical Society.

EDITED BY

EDWARD L. SCHAUB

THE OPEN COURT PUBLISHING COMPANY

CHICAGO   1936   LONDON

PRINTED IN THE UNITED STATES OF AMERICA

INTRODUCTION

At the thirty-fourth (1933) annual meeting of the Western Division of the American Philosophical Association a motion was passed creating the William Torrey Harris Centennial Committee, the main function of which was to be the planning of a suitable program to commemorate in 1935 the one-hundredth anniversary of the birth of Dr. Harris. Subsequently President J. D. Stoops appointed Professors Daniel S. Robinson, Charles M. Perry, and C. E. Cory members of the committee and designated Professor Robinson as chairman. It was later decided to hold the thirty-sixth (1935) annual meeting of the Western Division at Washington University, St. Louis, and to devote the opening sessions to a program honoring Dr. Harris.

After arranging a suitable program the committee decided that it would be fitting to publish the papers prepared especially for this meeting, along with biographical material. In carrying out this plan they invited Dr. Henry R. Evans, an intimate friend and former private secretary of Dr. Harris who now resides in Washington, D. C. to prepare an appreciative memoir for inclusion in the memorial volume. They also asked Professor H. G. Townsend to write especially for the volume an essay on "The Political Philosophy of Hegel in a Frontier Society," since circumstances prevented his attending the meeting in St. Louis and since he was especially well qualified to discuss this subject. We are sure that informed readers will agree that his contribution is essential to an adequate understanding of Dr. Harris' philosophy.

Dr. Evans' memoir, Professor Townsend's essay and the

papers presented at the St. Louis meeting comprise this memorial volume. The Committee is especially grateful to the Open Court Publishing Company for their splendid coöperation in making possible the publication of this important material on Dr. Harris, who undoubtedly deserves a high rank among the American philosophers of the last half of the nineteenth century. It is hoped that future historians of American culture and philosophy may find herein valuable source material. A complete bibliography of Dr. Harris' writings has been published by the United States Government Office of Education and has been reprinted in a somewhat abbreviated form by Professor Charles M. Perry in his *The St. Louis Movement in Philosophy* Since this bibliography is already available, the committee invited Dr. Leidecker to prepare a supplementary bibliography of books and articles about Dr. Harris, many of which have been published since the other list was prepared. We owe to Dr. Evans the rare photograph of Dr. Harris reproduced as a frontispiece. It is the photograph used by the artist who painted the picture which hangs in the Office of the Commissioner of Education in Washington, D. C.

D. S. ROBINSON,

C. E. CORY,

CHARLES M. PERRY,

Harris Centennial Committee.

CONTENTS

WILLIAM TORREY HARRIS: AN APPRECIATION

BY HENRY RIDGLEY EVANS

La Rochefoucauld says that no man is a hero to his valet. A man may not be a hero to his valet, but he very frequently is to his private secretary, as witness the magnificent tribute to Lincoln by his secretaries, Nicolay and Hay, in their biography of the famous emancipator.

It was my great good fortune in the year 1889 to become private secretary to Dr. William Torrey Harris, educator and philosopher, who for seventeen years presided over the destinies of the Bureau of Education, now the Office of Education, of the United States Department of the Interior.

Doctor Harris had recently returned from France, where he had represented the Bureau at the Paris Exposition. President Harrison had appointed him Commissioner of Education of the United States, which position he held until the year 1906. By a lucky turn of Fortune's wheel I served Doctor Harris as private secretary for three years, and he became my hero. He frequently invited me to his home on Columbia Heights, Washington, D. C., to meet such men as F. B. Sanborn, Denton J. Snider, Henry C. Brokmeyer,* and Thomas Davidson. On these memorable occasions I heard some very illuminating discussions on philosophy, ethics, religion, art, and sociology. Brokmeyer, erstwhile Lieutenant Governor of Missouri, was a student of Kant and Hegel. He is the author of *Letters on Faust*. Snider's commentaries on Shakespeare's plays had given him a world-wide repu-

---

* With reference to the spelling of his name see Harvey Gates Townsend, *Philosophical Ideas in the United States,* p. 116, n. 1.—*Ed.*

tation. Davidson was an authority on ancient Greek life and philosophy. His clashes with Doctor Harris over Aristotle and Aquinas were worth going miles to hear. Truly were these men intellectual giants. I profited much by these symposiums. It was like sitting at the feet of Plato to hear Doctor Harris discourse on "divine philosophy."

Plato was so named, it is said, because of his broad shoulders. Who can forget the magnificent breadth of Doctor Harris' shoulders? In the lobby of the Bureau, on the second floor, was a bust of Plato. I once called Doctor Harris' attention to the resemblance between himself and the plaster-of-Paris replica of the Grecian sage. "Although that cast is labeled 'Plato,'" he answered, "I am not so certain about its being an authentic portrait. I have seen the original marble in the Louvre, at Paris. Archeologists differ in opinion about it. Some say that it is a bust of Bacchus!" "Hardly that," I expostulated, somewhat chagrined. He laughed heartily, like a big school boy, slapped me on the back, and begged me not to take the matter too seriously.

A more kindly hearted man never lived than Doctor Harris. He was charity personified. No case of want or suffering that came to his attention was ever passed unnoticed. His life was characterized by simplicity and goodness of heart. As Ben Blewett has well said of him: "He was a lover of his fellow men, and especially delighted in stimulating to their highest capacity those associated with him in companionship or work." No matter how busy he might be with the routine duties of the office, he was ever ready to lay down his work to listen patiently to anyone who might call upon him for aid, financial or intellectual. He did not know the meaning of the word "envy," but scattered everywhere his wealth of knowledge. The Bureau of Education became the Mecca of aspirants to philosophical fame. Like Carlyle, his idea was "to produce, to produce."

He said to me one day: "If you have any thoughts to give to the world which you consider of value, get them printed; disseminate them. My own plan of doing this, when I was unknown to the reading world, was to get my essays published, no matter how obscure the journal in which they appeared. I asked no compensation for them, other than a few hundred reprints, which I scattered among those interested in education, art, and philosophy. Before long authors were sending me their own lucubrations. By such means I established associations and came into touch with the thinking men the world over."

William Torrey Harris was born at North Killingly, Conn., on September 10, 1835. He was the son of William and Zilpah (Torrey) Harris. His father was a farmer in comfortable circumstances. His colonial paternal ancestor was Thomas Harris, who, in 1630, sailed from Bristol, England, with Roger Williams in the good ship *Lyon*, landed at Salem, Mass., and in 1637 settled at Providence, R. I. The maternal grandparents of Doctor Harris were William and Zilpah (Davidson) Torrey, the former a descendant of William Torrey, a native of Combe St. Nicholas, Somersetshire, England, who emigrated in 1640, settled at Weymouth, Mass., became "captain of the Trainband," and was a member of the committee to examine Eliot's Bible.

Doctor Harris received his preparatory training at Woodstock (Conn.) Academy and Phillips Academy, Andover, Mass. He entered Yale College in the class of 1858, but after spending two and a half years at that seat of learning he removed in 1857 to St. Louis, Mo., where he began his professional career as a teacher of shorthand. In 1858 he became an assistant teacher in the public schools of St. Louis, rising eventually to superintendent of city schools, holding the latter position from 1867 to 1880.

It was in St. Louis that he came in contact with Henry C. Brokmeyer, one of the young men who emigrated to America "in a reflex movement growing out of the political troubles in Germany in the previous decade." Says F. A. Fitzpatrick, in the *Educational Review* for January, 1910: "Brokmeyer was a student of Kant, and an enthusiastic admirer of Hegel. Fresh from his studies, he became actuated with the spirit of modernism, of vocationalism, and determined to learn a trade. He selected that of a stove-molder; later, influenced by Thoreau, he lived as a hermit in the woods; then, reinvigorated, returned to St. Louis to enter the practice of law. He raised a regiment which served through the Civil War, and earned in later years the plaudits of all good citizens for his rugged honesty and his intellectual insight. It was during Brokmeyer's career as a stove-molder that Ira Divoll, W. T. Harris, and Holland discovered him and his knowledge of Kant and Hegel. They made frequent visits to Brokmeyer's room on the 'East Side' of St. Louis, often arriving before Brokmeyer had cooked his frugal meal and while he was physically worn out by his labors. The enthusiasm of this little band of students in a new and materialistic atmosphere, seeking light upon the obscure passages and involved construction of Kant's *Critique of Pure Reason,* echoed the ardor and interest of the students of Greek in the fifteenth century, as chronicled by Symonds in the story of the rise of the Italian republics. To Doctor Harris this study meant going over again his Aristotle and his Plato. He mastered the dialectic, and shutting out the rest of the world, for a period he became self-hypnotized by the ontological reveries of Hegel. How he managed to find the time for this study is a mystery to me even now, for at this time Doctor Harris, with Graham, the author of a revised Pitmanic shorthand system, taught stenography in their evening school in St. Louis, the first school of the kind west of New York. Quite a number of able newspaper men learned stenography at this school."

The little band of students in St. Louis practically inaugurated the philosophical movement in the United States.

In 1867 Doctor Harris founded the *Journal of Speculative Philosophy,* the first attempt of its kind in America. Twenty-two volumes appeared, the last of which was published in 1893. Into this journal were poured the brilliant essays of many noted men. Brokmeyer and others translated for it the best thoughts of the German metaphysicians. Those who possess a set of the *Journal of Speculative Philosophy* are indeed fortunate. Under the editorship of Doctor Harris it attracted the attention of great European thinkers. In the year 1879 Doctor Harris, Thomas Davidson, A. Bronson Alcott, Ralph Waldo Emerson, and F. B. Sanborn founded the Concord School of Philosophy, at Concord, Mass. What the members of this group sought in their discussions at Concord was not "an absolute unity of opinion, but a general agreement in the manner of viewing philosophic truth and applying it to the problems of life."

In the year 1880 Doctor Harris resigned from the St. Louis schools and devoted himself to lecturing on pedagogy, and the pursuit of literature. In the year 1889 he became, as already stated, United States Commissioner of Education.

Doctor Harris, though nominally a Republican in politics, was not a "hide-bound" member of that political faith. In fact, some of the newspapers of the eighties accused him of being a "mug-whump"— a political phrase much in vogue in that period. It seems that he had conscientious scruples on being appointed Commissioner of Education by President Harrison when he had voted for President Cleveland. Harrison, a broad-minded and liberal man, replied that it did not make any difference and urged him to accept the office which he did, as previously noted. Four years later Cleveland defeated Harrison and renewed the appointment of Doctor Harris, whereupon the latter informed Cleveland that he felt reluctant to accept the office of the Commissioner of Education as he had voted for Harrison; and Cleveland, like his predecessor, replied that it did not make any difference. The foregoing shows the admiration and esteem in which Doctor Harris was held.

In 1906 he resigned from the Government service and retired to Providence, R. I., where he died on November 5, 1909. He was buried at Putnam Heights (North Killingly), Conn. On his monument is the following quotation from Goethe's *Tribute to Plato:* "A rare scholar whose life was zealously and untiringly devoted to philosophy and education. His relation to the world is that of a superior spirit. . . . All that he utters has a reference to something complete, good, true, beautiful, whose furtherance he strives to promote in every bosom."

Doctor Harris left a widow, Sarah, daughter of James Bugbee, of Thompson, Conn., to whom he was married on December 27, 1858, and two children, Theodore and Edith

Davidson Harris. The Carnegie Foundation for the Advancement of Teaching conferred upon him, "as the first man to whom such recognition for meritorious service is given, the highest retiring allowance which our rules will allow, an annual income of $3,000." Orders were conferred upon him by the French and Italian Governments, and many great universities of Europe and America gave him honorary degrees. The famous old University of Jena, where Fichte, Schelling, Hegel, and Oken held forth in philosophy and Schiller lectured in history, conferred upon him the degree of doctor of philosophy in 1889. In 1894 he received from the King of Italy the chivalric decoration of Commander of the Order of Mauritius and Lazarus. The French Government in 1878 conferred upon him the honorary title of Officer of the Academy, and in 1889 the title of Officer of Public Instruction.

"In personal contact," says a writer in the National Cyclopedia of American Biography, "Doctor Harris was a perpetual flood and flow of light by tongue and pen. He was the indefatigable torchbearer of high philosophy and was forever lighting up those four great watchtowers, Kant, Hegel, Aristotle, and Plato, holding their importance in the order named." He was the author of *The Spiritual Sense of Dante's Divina Commedia* (1889); *Introduction to the Study of Philosophy* (1889); *Hegel's Logic* (1890); *Psychologic Foundations of Education* (1898); chapters on the philosophy of A. Bronson Alcott, in Sanborn's *Memoir of Alcott* (1893); and of many brochures on art, education, and philosophy. He was the editor-in-chief of Webster's International Dictionary; also the editor of Appleton's International Education Series.

"He was," says Fitzpatrick, "deeply religious in spirit, what might be termed intellectually a Christian. He seemed to have approached religion from the intellectual side, and not from the side of faith. He was fond of showing how certain dogmas of the Christian world, usually accepted through faith, were to him intellectually demonstrated."

Doctor Harris' most notable contribution to philosophy was his *Hegel's Logic,* written for Grigg's philosophical classics. The keynote of his insight is the doctrine of "self-activity." In his essay on Emerson he says: "Plato may stand for the philosophic seer of all time—Plato or Aristotle, it makes little difference which; for Aristotle reaffirms the same doctrine, and proceeds to show in detail the explanation of nature and man, as the revelation of divine reason. That the ultimate presupposition of all science is a personal first cause or absolute reason is evident to the philosopher who has learned to think in the school of Plato and Aristotle, or in the schools of their greatest followers; it is seen to be implied in the fact that the One from whence all proceeds is necessarily self-active and self-determined. Even if it is called *water,* or *air,* or *matter* as first principle, it must be *causa sui.* All things are to be explained as produced by its activity, and as growing or perishing through it. The self-determined is both subject and object of its activity, and this must be identified as mind — or has been thus identified by the thinkers mentioned who follow Aristotle or Plato."

Doctor Harris, strictly speaking, did not enunciate any new principle in philosophy, but, like Plato and Aristotle, laid emphasis on the doctrine of self-activity. To anyone who thinks with any degree of profundity, it is an axiom that the "self-active" and the "self-determined" are akin to mind and will. All the material forces of nature are moved by the impact of other forces, and so on *ad infinitum.*

Only a self-activity can start an initial movement when everything is reduced to a state of complete equilibrium. The orderly evolution of the universe from chaos is the product of intelligence or mind. "God geometrizes," says Plato. Man did not invent mathematics; he discovered it in the very essence of things. Doctor Harris was continually hammering at the iron heated in the furnace of self-activity, for he saw with clear vision that anyone who possesses an insight into this fundamental principle of philosophy has reached the very bedrock of thinking.

Doctor Harris' philosophy of pedagogy is to be explained by this doctrine of the "self-active." The universe is not directed by "a blind, unconscious force," but by divine reason, mind. "A spiritual first principle," he writes, "makes mind the source of the universe and the explanation of nature and history. Mind is consciousness, personality, will, intellect, love. In the absolute personality, intellect and will and love are one, because each in its perfection is all. The absolute self-knowledge which makes of itself an object thereby creates, or is, absolute will. But its self-made object is also one with it by love and recognition. Hence Plato called his first principle the good, inasmuch as he wished to indicate that it is a will in accordance with reason, and not a blind will, such as Schopenhauer sets up and Buddhism presupposes. Plato's God creates the world as 'like himself as possible,' for 'no goodness can have envy of anything.' Hence nature must be a revelation of infinite goodness, and man must have a divine origin and a divine destiny."

Doctor Harris' scheme of pedagogy becomes luminous after reading the foregoing. Man is indeed a self-active entity, the master of his own fate, and not the idle sport of chance, called into being by "a fortuitous collocation of atoms." "All below man," he says in his *Philosophy in Outline,* "pass away and do not retain individuality. Man is self-determining as an individual, and hence includes his own development within himself as an individual, and hence is immortal and free." Education should endeavor to prepare him to understand the view of the world entertained by his civilization; to put him into possession of the wisdom of the race; to cultivate character, spirituality, and the social ideal; it should not consist merely in taking care of the body and in the performance of the lower social functions — the preparation of food, clothing, and shelter — though these are of importance in the general rounding out of man. With Herbert Spencer's pantheistic philosophy Doctor Harris had little patience, and still less with the great agnostic's educational theories.

Doctor Harris was an omnivorous reader. Of Goethe's *Wilhelm Meister* he said to me: "I endeavor to re-read *Wilhelm Meister* every year, and always find it more suggestive than before. It has increased my practical power tenfold." Carlyle's *The French Revolution* and *Frederick the Great* he pronounced the "greatest epic poems since Homer's *Iliad*." He was a devoted admirer of Sir Walter Scott's novels, but he proclaimed Victor Hugo's *Les Misérables* the greatest work of fiction of the nineteenth century — perhaps of any century.

It is interesting to note that just before he died Doctor Harris was putting the finishing touches to a book on *Courses of Study,* the manuscript of which he loaned to a friend, who lost it on a railroad train. In his literary work he never let anything go out of his hands without, as he expressed it, "letting it soak." He polished it continually. This perhaps accounts for the fact of his producing but few books, though his pamphlet literature is legion. One of his most inspiring works is *The Spiritual Sense of Dante's Divina Commedia.* He says, "Of all the great world poems, unquestionably Dante's Divina Commedia may be justly claimed to have a spiritual sense, for it possesses a philosophic system and admits of allegorical interpretation. It is par excellence the religious poem of the world."

In *The Chautauquan,* during 1881-82, Doctor Harris published his masterly treatise on "Christianity in Art," which is a discussion of "the nature of art and its five special forms — architecture, sculpture, painting, music, and poetry." He intended to issue the foregoing in book form, handsomely illustrated, but never could find the time to re-edit and prepare the material for the press.

Doctor Harris worked like the proverbial steam engine, day and night. His splendid physique enabled him to stand a strain that would have killed most men long before the allotted span. He slept comparatively little. I frequently dined at his home, and have seen him carry some abstruse volume to the table. His food lay almost untouched before him; he simply nibbled at it, so absorbed was he in the book. He died leaving the world richer by his having lived.

Doctor Harris was a man of almost encyclopedic knowledge, and under his leadership the Bureau of Education acquired a prestige among educators and philosophers in America and Europe that it had never before known; it was largely "the lengthened shadow of a man." To quote from the brochure on the Bureau by Darrell H. Smith: "The seventeen years of his commissionership reveal an intellect that won wide admiration, an inspirational leadership of undoubted value, aims and ideals of the highest type. But it is the individual who stands out, and not the organization. Doctor Harris takes rank today as one of the nation's great educational leaders, but his abilities did not extend to the management of administrative machinery." [1]

Doctor Harris' conception of the purpose of the Bureau is thus summed up by him: [2] "The legitimate function of the Bureau of Education is the collection and distribution of educational information. Each place should know the fruits of experience in all other places. A national bureau should not merely collect the statistics of education in the several States, but should also study the systems established by the various nations of Europe and Asia. Doubtless each nation has devised some kind of discipline, some course of study, which will train the children of its schools into habits in harmony with its laws. An investigation of these features in view of the obvious demands of the governmental forms will furnish us with a science of comparative pedagogy."

It was under Doctor Harris' administration that European systems of education were thoroughly and systematically studied and evaluated, not only from an historical, but also from a practical standpoint. In his first annual report, 1888-89, he presented a comparative study of the educational systems of the United States, Germany, France, Italy, and Spain, illustrated with statistical graphs. From that period to the present time the administrative changes and pedagogical movements in foreign countries have been stressed in publications of the Bureau. To a certain extent this information had been given in reports of Doctor Harris' predecessors, but it was not presented in such elaborate and analytical form.

---

1 D. H. Smith, *The Bureau of Education,* etc. (Johns Hopkins Press, 1923), p. 15.

2 *Annual Report of the Commissioner.* 1888-89, Vol. I, p. xix.

Doctor Harris' introductions to his annual reports were distinguished by rare pedagogical insight and were appreciated by schoolmen. He also put the statistics of the Bureau on a thoroughly scientific basis, for he was expert in that field, and held frequent conferences with men noted as specialists in statistics, such as, for example, Carroll D. Wright, who at that time was Commissioner of Labor of the United States.

The appropriation for salaries during the administration of Doctor Harris increased from $45,420 in 1899 to $53,140 for 1906. In 1902 the salary of the commissioner was raised from $3,000 to $3,500. It might have been more, but Doctor Harris had a natural antipathy to asking Congress for funds, and this antipathy put him out of touch with the Appropriations Committee of the House when it came to the question of the general expansion of the Bureau. He was preëminently the scholar, the philosopher of education, and did not care overmuch for the administrative details of office. Doctor Harris carried on a large correspondence with leaders of educational and philosophical thought in this and foreign countries and was most active in contributing to pedagogical journals. A complete bibliography of his writings, which I prepared under his supervision, is contained in the *Annual Report of the Commissioner of Education,* 1907, Volume I, pages 37-72.[3]

The most comprehensive evaluation of the intellectual labors of Doctor Harris is contained in *William T. Harris: A Critical Study of His Educational and Related Philosophical Views,* by Dr. John S. Roberts, District Superintendent of Schools, New York City. This work is pub-

---

3 Republished in pp. 96-148 of *The St. Louis Movement in Philosophy: Some Source Material,* ed. by C. M. Perry, Norman, Univ. of Okla. Press, 1930.

lished by the National Education Association, of which
Doctor Harris was a life director and its president in 1875.
Says Doctor Roberts: "To interpret and appreciate the
writings of Doctor Harris, the student must have in mind
the most important truths of the great idealistic philosophers — Socrates, Plato, Aristotle, Leibnitz, The Church
Fathers, Kant, Fichte, Schelling, Hegel, and Rosenkranz.
Their views of the world were the views accepted by Doctor Harris. 'They were thinkers, deep, mighty thinkers,'
he said. (*Journal of Speculative Philosophy,* Vol. 19.)
He, too, was a deep, mighty thinker and had studied and
absorbed their teachings. The most direct influence on
his thoughts, especially in relation to education, was exercised by the writings of Hegel and Rosenkranz. Of Hegel
he said, in 1908, 'I have now commenced the reading of
Hegel's *Philosophy of History* for the seventeenth time,
and I shall get more out of it at this reading than at any
previous one.' (*Proceedings of the National Education
Association,* 1910, p. 92.)

"But he was just as familiar with the writings of other
philosophers and was able to show clearly the fallacies of
the materialistic and mechanistic writers. He was the
constant and bitter foe of the Atomists, the Sophists, the
Brahmanistic philosophers, the Eleatics, Spinoza, Hamilton, Hume, Rousseau, Herbert Spencer, and all others
whose theories led, in his opinion, to materialism, pantheism, agnosticism, and atheism.

"He sought to learn the deepest thoughts of the greatest workers in all fields, to understand the genesis and interrelation of their ideas, to distinguish between those doctrines that were transient and those that were fundamental and everlasting, and to apply the basic truths to all
forms of human life and civilized institutions."

WILLIAM T. HARRIS AND THE EARLY HISTORY OF THE INDIANA STATE NORMAL SCHOOL

BY WILLIAM LOWE BRYAN

The story of the influence of a certain form of the philosophy of Hegel upon thousands of teachers in Indiana in the last quarter of the last century through the agency of the Indiana State Normal School at Terre Haute is of great interest from many points of view.

I believe that the Hegel influence came to that School primarily through its first president, William A. Jones. I wish I knew, as I do not, from what man or book President Jones derived his Hegel. He must have been a man of great force of mind and personality because in the very few years of his presidency he made an impression which was still profound twenty-five years after his departure upon thousands who never knew him.

His first pupils in the philosophy to which he was devoted were the members of his first faculty. One of them, Professor Cyrus Hodgin, later of Earlham College, has told me that it was a common occurrence for President Jones to call his small faculty together on a Monday, after a week-end of meditation, and say "I have had a revelation. I wish you to consider it with me." This meant that he had a fresh-born Hegelian idea which he wished each man in the faculty to find a way of using in the development of his subject.

Jones' philosophy was anything but a cut-and-dried system either for him or for his faculty. His philosophy was alive and growing continuously. He laid his mind upon his faculty and he laid his mind far more profoundly upon the best of his students. These younger men came to be the faculty of the School, and as long as they lived Hegel was coming through Jones and through his pupils (Parsons, Sandison, Tompkins, and others) to successive generations of Normal School students for whom a certain adumbration of Hegel became a philosophy of life and more or less a religion.

Contemporary American students of Hegel could not but be deeply interested in this extraordinary social phenomenon. One of them, Denton J. Snider, came often to the School to give courses in which he expounded his Hegelian interpretations of Homer, Dante, Goethe, and Shakespeare. And often Dr. William T. Harris came to see the extraordinary flowering of Hegelian ideas where it might have been least expected. His visits must have given invaluable guidance and inspiration to the men who were in charge of the School.

I came to know those men with respect in the later years of their service. President Parsons had the powerful mind and will of a man of affairs. He was a man who as lawyer, banker, or senator could have held his own with the best. Arnold Tompkins, cheerful, witty, with simple untechnical language would lure students and audiences as if he were the Pied Piper. And always he was luring them into discipleship with Hegel — that is, with his Hegel.

Howard Sandison would seem dry or even dull as he went on from the first premise of the first day in the year to the overwhelming conclusion of the last day in the year. But consider what was happening within the minds of his students. Because they were held incessantly and intensively to a logic which seemed as inevitable as calculus, those students not only arrived with Sandison at his conclusion but their minds were made to think in his forms about every subject whatever. Only those who through years pursue a system of theology from its form in a child catechism to its form in a metaphysical system are made over through and through as Sandison's students were made over. So in a teacher's institute in a remote corner of Indiana you might hear an ardent great-great-great grandchild of Hegel expounding the inevitable way of teaching English grammar or cube root.

Of course there were many who got some of the words with only a distant glimmer of the meanings. I remember one hopelessly dull man who was never done talking of the Absolute, as with another upbringing he might have sought to expound Calvin or Spinoza. I remember one of his disgusted colleagues, who hated Hegel and all his works, saying "Old ———— is certainly hell on the Absolute."

I understand that there is in preparation a history of the Indiana State Normal School, now called the Indiana State Teachers College. There still survive men who were part of its first quarter-century. Those men know the inside of the story as I can not. I look with great interest for the appearance of this story of a notable chapter in American social history.

Reverting to Dr. Harris, it is not necessary for me to say anything here of his work as a philosopher. I note, however, that he who adventured as philosopher as far as Dante did into the depths of hell and the heights of paradise was a most alert resident of this actual world. He knew how to deal with men in the interest of his high purposes as effectively as the shrewdest Yankee, for he was Yankee before he was philosopher. He used to control the decisions of the National Education Association year after year as a President of the United States aspires to control and seldom does control the decisions of Congress. When Dr. Harris said thumbs up on any proposal in the Association it was adopted. When he said thumbs down, that idea was dead as a dodo. Well, they always thought he must be right whether they understood what he was saying or not. I heard him often at Indiana University and elsewhere. I have sat in a group about him and heard his shrewd sense, his keen wit, or his flight into the stratosphere of philosophic thought. A great American. A great man.

THE ST. LOUIS PHILOSOPHICAL MOVEMENT

BY GEORGE ROWLAND DODSON

The St. Louis Philosophical Movement which began in 1859 when the systematic study of Hegel was undertaken by Henry C. Brokmeyer, Wm. T. Harris, and a few others and which may be said to have ended in 1893, when the *Journal of Speculative Philosophy* ceased to be published, was a striking and significant episode in the history of American thought. First of all, it was a lay movement. This was unusual, for philosophy is ordinarily a professional enterprise. Its devotees have become a caste. They study to become teachers of the subject. Their pupils in turn become professors of philosophy and those whom they instruct teach others in turn; thus arises a sort of apostolic succession.

The St. Louis Movement was not of this kind, though most of its leaders were college men, academic in type and thought. At least one of them, Thomas Davidson, was a distinguished scholar. The Movement awakened and held the interest of a considerable number of men and women of intellectual power who were important leaders in politics, education, and in the general culture of their time. They felt that philosophy has a public service to perform. It was not mainly an affair of professors. Rather was its function to make clear the great thoughts that help us to live. To live well, every thoughtful man needs a comprehensive view of life which will help him to get and to keep his bearings in the world. To be of use, of value, philosophy must be not only a *Weltanschauung*, but also a *Lebensweisheit*.

The men and women who were identified with the St. Louis movement would not have been interested in many of the technical and abstract discussions which have a place in meetings of the American Philosophical Association. With some tendencies in the philosophizing of the present day, they would have had little sympathy; for instance, with the aspiration to be scientific, as physics is scientific. This is ruinous in all departments of intellectual activity except the physical sciences, that is, in ethics, aesthetics, philosophy of religion, and perhaps also in psychology, sociology, and economics. For science means precision and this is possible only through measurement, and the great values of life, Truth, Beauty, and Goodness, cannot be measured. It follows that while we can be intelligent with regard to them, we cannot deal profitably with them through the concepts of physics. Professor Schiller speaks of philosophies which seem to cultivate technicality for its own sake. They often make a great parade of exactness, but soon get lost in a vast apparatus of definitions and distinctions which involve the learning of a great variety of uncouth dialects.

In a paper which I read in St. Louis before the Western Philosophical Association twenty-six years ago, I tried to answer the following questions: What were the elements in Kant and Hegel which made them appeal to a group of western Americans in the middle of the nineteenth century? Why did a number of men of ability in this country find a sort of gospel in Hegel at a time when his philosophy was discredited and neglected in the land of its birth? Why did their propaganda have so considerable a measure of success, and why were these enthusiastic students of idealistic philosophy themselves so successful in practical affairs? The answer to these questions lies almost on the surface. Continued investigation only confirms the first impression.

In the first place we may well consider why it is that any philosophical or religious movement succeeds. The obvious answer is that the philosophy or religion in question satisfies yearnings, cravings, and profound needs. Harnack in his *Expansion of Christianity,* shows that one of the causes of the success of primitive Christianity was the irruption of Syrian and Persian religions into the Roman empire. These movements stirred up new religious cravings which could not be satisfied apart from Christianity.

If now we turn to Vol. I, No. 1, of the *Journal of Speculative Philosophy* we find on the first page the leading motive of the St. Louis Philosophical Movement clearly stated by Dr. Harris. "There is no need," he says, "to speak of the immense religious movements now going on in this country and in England. The tendency to break with the traditional and to accept only what bears for the soul its own justification, is widely active and can end only in the demand that reason shall find and establish a philosophical basis for all those great ideas which are taught as religious dogmas. Thus it is that side by side with the naturalism of such men as Renan, a school of mystics is beginning to spring up who prefer to ignore utterly all historical wrappages and cling only to the speculative kernel itself. The vortex between the traditional faith and the intellectual conviction cannot be closed by renouncing the latter, but only by deepening it to speculative insight."

That is, neither naturalism nor mysticism satisfies. While we cannot accept tradition unmodified, our instinct for history will not allow us to break with it altogether.

The leaders of the St. Louis Movement were men whose
soul life had been nourished on Christian conceptions and
it was not strange that they should seek for an interpretation which would make it possible for them, without
losing their intellectual integrity, to accept the facts of
science and to maintain their hold on a spiritual movement in which they felt there is a treasure of immeasur-
able value.

The craving for science is strong but men who also
yearn to believe in God, Freedom, and Immortality, inevitably seek to escape the philosophy of Naturalism which
science was at that time supposed to involve. The crisis
was by many minds acutely felt. How William James
suffered from it is evident from his letters. Thus he writes
in 1896,—"I take it that no man is educated who has
never dallied with the thought of suicide." [1] And in 1868
at the age of twenty-five, he writes to T. W. Ward, "all
last winter when I was on the continual verge of suicide,
it used to amuse me to hear you chaff my animal con-
tentment." [2] So it comes out that when he was describing
"the sick soul," James was speaking from experience. Professor F. C. Schiller diagnoses James' depression as follows: [3] "A comparison of these documents shows, I think,
that the essential trouble with James, as with so many of
his generation, was the withering of the spiritual values,
of God, freedom, and immortality, under the devastating
onset of Naturalism. Nowadays some have learnt, from
James as much as from any one, that the situation is by
no means desperate, while many, it is to be feared, have
grown used to their spiritual losses, and no longer view

---

[1] *The Letters of William James,* ed. by Henry James (Boston, 1926),
Vol. II, p. 39.

[2] *Ibid.,* Vol. I, p. 129.

[3] In his *Must Philosophers Disagree,* p. 89.

them tragically. But at that time Naturalism seemed to bear down all opposition with the irresistible might of science, and to leave nothing standing but the meaningless evolutions of matter determined by a mindless mechanism. This view of the world had received an imposing systematic form in the Synthetic Philosophy of Herbert Spencer, whose vogue was even greater in America than in England. Against it James' soul revolted."

There are still many minds which are distressed by a situation in which "the things we care for most are at the mercy of the things we care for least." If, however, these souls with frustrated religious longings are fewer today, the fact is susceptible of explanation. Naturalism, for instance, is no longer the bogey it once was. We see clearly now, what almost no one saw six or seven decades ago, namely, that mechanism is an excellent, even indispensable, hypothesis in scientific research, but miserably inadequate as a philosophy. As a metaphysics it is falling into disrepute. We find some mechanism in many parts of the cosmos, but we have discovered nothing to justify the negative conclusion that there is nothing but mechanism in the universe.

Another fact helps to illuminate the situation. A clear distinction is now more generally made than at the time when the St. Louis Philosophical Movement began. This distinction, which has justly been called one of the great achievements of the nineteenth century, is that "between religion itself, on the one hand, and the expression of religion in doctrines and rites, or the application of religion through institutions, on the other." [4] This great idea has been to a certain extent popularized. We distinguish between the transient and the permanent in historic religion.

---

[4] E. C. Moore, *Christian Thought Since Kant*, p. 6.

Thanks to the service of great thinkers we no longer confuse the essential reality with the accidents, the kernel with the husk. In the days when Brokmeyer and Harris were young men there existed an unhappy situation which has been concisely described by Professor A. C. McGiffert, as follows: "The religious crisis was acute. Either a medieval man and a Christian, or a modern man and a skeptic —this seemed the sole alternative as viewed by many of the clearest-headed thinkers of the day." [5] Now, thanks to the St. Louis Philosophical Movement and to the influence of many scholars in other circles and associations, the situation is completely changed. As Professor McGiffert says, "New conceptions of religion have emerged and have resulted in forms of Christianity congenial to the temper and discoveries of the modern age, so that it has become possible for a man to be fully in sympathy with the modern spirit and yet remain a Christian." [6]

What was for Harris in 1860 a desideratum which would satisfy at once both philosophic and religious need is becoming a common possession. The problem as he saw it then is clearly stated in the second volume of the *Journal:* "This absolute truth, embodied in such a form as to be lived and felt as religion, should also be thought as pure truth."

It is to be noted that the St. Louis Philosophical Movement was not purely Hegelian nor even wholly philosophical. It was to a large extent a manifestation of an awakening interest in classical art and literature. One of the most striking figures associated with Dr. Harris was Denton J. Snider, a pure intellectual type whose great enthusiasm for the things of the mind was contagious. Through

---

5 A. C. McGiffert, *Protestant Thought Before Kant*, p. 253,.
6 *Ibid.*, p. 254.

him many people have become interested in Homer,
Dante, Shakespeare, and Goethe.   He wrote fifty books
and conducted many classes.   His disciples and friends
still maintain an association for universal culture and
annually make a pilgrimage to his grave.   The needs
served by the leaders of the Movement are now met by
colleges and universities, by extension lectures, by literary
clubs and societies.   What was once a swift and narrow
stream has become wider as it flows.   Another cause of
the decline of the Movement was the migration of some
of its leaders to other cities.   Dr. Harris gave much time
to the Concord School of Philosophy, Snider taught psychology in Chicago, Professor George H. Howison
accepted a call to the University of California, where he
became one of the most active and influential forces in the
intellectual life of the Pacific coast.

One of the most striking features of the Movement
was the deep feeling that philosophy is the most practical
of all species of knowledge.   In fact, these leaders were
successful.   Brokmeyer became Governor; Harris, Superintendent of Schools in St. Louis and then United States Commissioner of Education; Thomas Davidson was knight-
errant of the intellectual life; George H. Howison became
a distinguished philosopher on the Pacific Coast; Denton
J. Snider awakened many minds to the life of reflection.
Were these men successful not because of but in spite of
their philosophy?   I think not.   The Hegelian concepts,
of which the average American student tends to make
sport when he considers them at all, were amazingly useful in practical life.   There have been so many caricatures
of Hegelianism that the average thoughtful man despairs
of all who take his philosophy seriously, as of those who
have parted company with reality, who have left the road

to truth and are lost to all sane thinking forevermore.
Actually the intensely practical American mind is astonished to find that the reviled dialectic of Hegel is simply
a quaint statement of principles which he knows and applies intuitively and to which in large measure he owes
his practical success; for life is an art rather than a science; it is never the expression of a single principle but
always a conciliation of interests. It includes both egoistic
and altruistic tendencies. Some fail because they take
social oppositions to be absolute rather than as comple-
mentary. The successful man will be conciliatory. He
will not deny all reason to those who differ from him. He
will not beget irreconcilable antagonisms. Though an
enthusiastic reformer, he will not regard those who do
not fall in with his plans as the incarnation of evil. He is
too wise to take a principle and run away with it. For
unpractical and futile fanaticism, the vision of Hegel is
an effective cure.

That Hegel had a vision of the truth is explicitly admitted even by Professor James. He says that as a re-
porter of certain aspects of the actual, Hegel is great and
true. There is a dialectic movement in things and Hegel's
vision agrees with countless facts. Somehow life does
satisfy opposites at once. Hegel saw that to understand
anything we must see it in its relations. He knew that
all that is finite is provisional and that all objects and institutions are but phases of a process and that no antagonisms are absolute. Now, says James, Hegel's originality
lay in transporting the process from the sphere of per-
cepts to that of concepts.

All successful leaders and managers of men are in a
sense unconscious Hegelians. The art of life consists in
knowing how to conciliate interests in making the com-

promises which efficiency demands. It is easy to carica-
ture Hegel, but a certain amount of his philosophy is con-
ducive to moral integrity as well as to practical success;
it legitimates the compromises which success in practical
life requires, which we are all compelled to make, but
which, when we have no philosophy that gives this legiti-
mation, makes us reproach ourselves with inconsistency
and each other with hypocrisy. The Hegelian may make
an honest and efficient fight for the truth which he thinks
timely and important and yet with perfect sincerity recognize that those who are opposed to him are probably not
entirely without some right and reason on their side.

That Hegel, as the leaders of the St. Louis Movement
interpreted him, helped a good many people to live, is
probably not pure fancy. In the difficult task of living
together it would lessen friction and promote coöperation
if the eager promoters of special interests could learn and
apply the principle that to overemphasize any aspect of
truth is to get into a false position, that other standpoints
have their relative justification, that one may be conciliatory and yet sincere, that the absolute tone in us mortals
is out of place, and that large-mindedness is as important
and necessary in moral and political life as in philosophy.

WILLIAM TORREY HARRIS AND THE ST. LOUIS MOVEMENT IN PHILOSOPHY

BY CHARLES M. PERRY

The St. Louis Movement in Philosophy can be understood only in the light of American civilization as a whole. It represents a phase of the conflict between naturalism and idealism.

From the beginning of American life a tendency toward naturalism was developing. The deists and the materialists of the eighteenth century hardly need mention in this connection. In the early nineteenth century came the uniformitarian geology of Sir Charles Lyell which set pious scientists to trying to harmonize geology and Genesis. Shortly after the middle of the century there appeared from abroad the *Origin of Species,* Spencer's *First Principles,* which in spite of its unknowable is essentially naturalistic, and Huxley's explanations of the evolutionary doctrine. Attending this advance in naturalistic theory a social change occurred. By a law akin to the second law of thermo-dynamics, as Henry Adams has suggested, the high points in American society tended to lose their high potential and sink to the level of the mass. Just as miracles yielded to naturalistic interpretation so unique individuals, groups, and classes were dissolved in the democratic process. The Civil War, in which St. Louis participated so intimately, marked a point in this breakdown of distinctive social institutions.

Over the ever-leveling expanse of American society, however, high winds and water spouts have occasionally passed, raising the surface to a higher potential for shorter or longer periods. Jonathan Edwards' fight against the effects of the "Half-way covenant" and Timothy Dwight's war against deism were illustrations of such disturbances. The transcendentalists, when they attacked a dead orthodoxy and middle-class ways of thinking and living, had the same effect. Laurens Hickok's appeal to Immanuel Kant to support a judgment day was another such case.[1] John Fiske's attempt to find religious comfort in Spencer's unknowable was another. When the descendants of the Puritans interpreted the "will to believe" as the "right to believe," they too were contending against the desolation of naturalism. And the same battle is going on when men build a local community or organize a society on the basis of some new doctrine in the face of democratic and naturalistic forces that tend to dissolve it and bring it down to the level of the general mass.

The St. Louis Movement in Philosophy illustrates this principle. The community of St. Louis had a distinctive commercial, industrial, and social life. It had a colorful population consisting of French, German, and native Americans — one could hear foreign language and eat foreign food; Mississippi steamboats tied up at its wharfs, and captains, pilots, theatrical impressarios, prominent journalists, and politicians mingled with its people. The city raised itself to a commanding height, made itself widely known, then began to lose its unique position. The steamboats left its wharfs; the pilots, the more picturesque gamblers, and the captains disappeared. The philosophical movement in close union with the life of the city took its own peculiar direction, rose to great influence, and then through inner conflict and attrition from outside be-

---

[1] Laurens Hickok, *Rational Psychology*, p. 717.

gan to dissipate its energies. The freshness and originality of its fighting days were gradually lost and the philosophers went to other haunts.

Why the social phenomenon of the St. Louis Movement occurred at St. Louis is not easy to determine. The
presence of a large German element doubtless had something to do with it. But why did not the movement take
place in Cincinnati or Milwaukee? Why did Brokmeyer
walk out of the woods into St. Louis rather than into half
a dozen other cities? Why did Harris come to St. Louis
to teach shorthand rather than to Detroit or Chicago?
Why did Snider engage by letter to teach in the School
of the Christian Brothers in that same city? I realize that
the reasons are all perfectly clear in the absolute mind but
from the plane of particularity the problem seems insolu-
ble. From this angle it looks more like a fortuitous con-
course of atoms. Perhaps the best we can do is to sug-
gest that winds of doctrine from Germany and similar
winds from New England crossed each other's paths in
St. Louis and caused a rotary motion which whirled a
goodly part of the population up into the empyrean.

The dominant principle of St. Louis philosophy was
Hegelian. When Brokmeyer met Harris in 1858 he had
already decided that Hegel was the philosopher to be
studied. In his *Mechanic's Diary* he said, "With self-
determination as the ultimate principle of the universe,
thought has arrived at totality, and therefore at true objective internality, and not merely the subjective internality that predicates concerning an external. Thought
is what is — the perennial, the external, and every determination thereof embodies or prefigures this, its nature.
It is the internal for which the external is evanescent. It
plays with form, for it itself is the substance, and the one

substance in and of all forms." [2] Again in the same book he says regarding Hegel's logic, "It is a strange book and attractive to me, on account of its noiselessness. Whenever the world within or without commences to brawl so loudly that I cannot hear my own voice, I take a journey into the realm of this primeval solitude." [3] In this book he found universal dialectic. "Vice is a determination, a negation: but to negate this negation through the process of moral reformation, the result is an affirmative virtue." [4] And in his letters on *Faust* he gave an Hegelian interpretation of that masterpiece.

Immediately after the meeting of the two men in 1858 Harris sent to Germany for a copy of Hegel's larger *Logic* in the original and his life-work was started.

It took Harris years to master this "book of fate" as it was later called. He records that in 1863 he arrived at an insight into "independent being." In 1864 he obtained an insight into the subordination of fate to freedom. In 1866 he distinguished the difference between comprehension and idea. In the latter year he read the larger *Logic* through in Brokmeyer's translation for the first time.[5] During the period of his practical activities the concepts of this philosophy continually cropped out. When Snider followed him to Concord he found him bombarding the audience with his heaviest philosophical artillery. In 1903 Harris was reading a paper before the American Philosophical Association on "Hegel's Voyage of Discovery." Hegel far more than Kant brought Harris God, Freedom, and Immortality.

---

[2] Henry Brokmeyer, *Mechanic's Dairy*, pub. by his son, E. C. Brokmeyer, 1910, p. 24.

[3] *Ibid.*, p. 55.

[4] *Ibid.*, p. 60.

[5] *Cf.* W. T. Harris, *Hegel's Logic*, pp. ix-xi.

The one next most influenced by the larger *Logic* was Snider. It exasperated him but he could not leave it alone. Though Snider never wrote on philosophy in the narrow sense and turned more and more to literature as time passed, all of his attitudes and his standards of literary criticism were determined by Hegel — Snider found a triadic structure in the *Midsummer Night's Dream* and in the *Tempest*. He records that the philosophy embraced by him and his friends was an idealism, "one that put stress upon Idea or Spirit as the primordial creative source of all things. It was a great and necessary discipline which trained us to see underneath the mighty phenomenal occurrences of the passing hour, and to probe to their original starting point, to their creative essence." [6] But though greatly affected by Hegel, Snider was the least committed of the three — he alone could view the movement with appraising detachment and humor.

Equally Hegelian in doctrine but not so close to the center of the movement were a number of others. Judge Gabriel Woerner used Hegel's philosophy to produce impressive treatises on the *American Law of Administration* and on the *American Law of Guardianship*. He wrote several plays also and a novel, *The Rebel's Daughter,* which revolved around the St. Louis Movement. William M. Bryant, among other literary activities, wrote upon immortality in the unmistakable spirit of Hegel and translated a part of Hegel's *Aesthetics*. Susan Blow, speaking in commemoration of Dr. Harris after his death, tells of the rapture of her first awakening under the influence of Harris' lecturing to the vision of Hegel: "So victoriously had the lecturer wrestled with Kant, Fichte, Schelling, and Hegel that in two hours of what still seems to me

6 D. J. Snider, *St. Louis Movement, etc.,* p. 27.

miraculous explanation he had kindled in the mind of one eager listener a light which revealed idealism delivered from Solipsism.. . . The open secret was revealed and I knew that I stood upon the delectable mountains and discerned from afar the shining pinnacles of the Eternal City. . . . That afternoon was a solemn crisis in my life. I beheld Eternal Reality. I was a novice admitted to a sacred fellowship." And farther on she writes, "Truth can never be packed in definitions and passed from one to another in spoken words. It is a light which spreads from mind to mind — a flame which spreads from heart to heart — a challenge which sounds from will to will." [7] In a less reverent mood Snider has described Miss Blow — the pioneer public school kindergartner — as using "ponderous Hegelian nomenclature" in explaining a "game of the babies." [8]

Among the others who belonged to the movement were some who were not Hegelian. The most prominent of these were Adolph Ernst Kroeger, the Fichtean; L. F. Soldan, who is listed by Snider as philosophically neutral; Professor George H. Howison of Washington University, who was committed to personal idealism; and, last but not least, Thomas Davidson. Snider has characterized Davidson as usually upholding "Aristotle as against Hegel, and even the Greek world against the Christian." "A lively and ingenious Scotchman," he says, "who never seemed to me to have any persistent conviction. At the time he was certainly a jolly drifter and general free fighter, with much effervescence of erudition." [9] It may be added to Snider's characterization that Davidson did not like the

---

[7] Susan Blow, "The Service of Dr. Harris to the Kindergarten," *Kindergarten Review*, June, 1910.

[8] D. J. Snider, *op. cit.*, p. 291.

[9] *Ibid.*, p. 33.

facile way in which the Hegelians synthesized their contradictions and arrived at unity. The relation between
him and Harris may be shown by a story told by Professor
Bakewell. Several of the philosophers of that time were
at Glenmore in the Adirondacks where Davidson was holding a summer school in philosophy. In one of their con-
versations Harris said, counting upon his fingers, "This
is the Father, this is the Son, and this is the Holy Spirit."
Davidson immediately interrupted, his irritation accentu-
ating his normal Scottish burr: "I have heard that a hundred times if I have heard it once, and I will *not* hear it
again." Whereupon Harris said, pointing to his fingers
again: "This is the Father, this is the Son, and this is the
Holy Spirit."

A second dominant characteristic of the St. Louis
Movement was that it centered around the public schools.
Transcendentalism found expression in the lyceum. The
Hegelian influence elsewhere in America was confined
entirely to academic institutions. The St. Louis group
were mostly teachers in the city schools. Harris was superintendent; Snider and Morgan were high-school in-
structors. Soldan was a later superintendent of schools;
Francis Cook was a school principal; Miss Blow, Miss
Fruchte and Miss Brackett were all connected with the
schools. It thus came about that the applications of philosophy were made mostly to teaching problems. The
fact that the movement was largely non-academic made
it take its place along with the chautauqua and similar
movements as the educator of those who had not had opportunities for higher education of a formal sort.

The question now to be answered is why was Harris
so outstanding in the group? It is customary to place
him second to Brokmeyer in philosophical insight. If he

is second he is certainly a close second. It is true that he
is not so dark and unintelligible as his leader but in this
latter regard he frequently attains nearly equal obscuri-
ties. Though his comprehension of Hegel came slowly
he gained an original and passionate insight into the philosophy of the master; every cell of his body and every
activity of his life were pervaded by it. It took complete
possession of him and made him a power in nearly every
relation. In assessing Harris' significance in the movement this fact should not be neglected.

A second factor determining his position was his amaz-
ing practical ability. This was emphasized by the fact
that most of the other members of the group did not possess this ability — they could think and debate and write
but could not organize on a large scale or maintain stable
social relations. Brokmeyer was highly gifted but so ex-
plosive that Harris did not dare to take him to Concord
to lecture, and when the management of the Literary
School in Milwaukee invited him to lecture there his tem-
perament made the occasion memorable. Snider was a
talented and lovable man but he had to be a free lance:
he would not submit to being edited and consequently had
to publish his works himself; he would not accept administrative responsibility or tie himself down to an academic
position. Miss Blow was a profound and brilliant woman
but if Snider's picture of her is true she was poorly ad-
justed to her social environment. Surely Davidson did
not possess administrative qualifications and if Howison
had them they did not show themselves in any eminent
degree at that time. This situation left Harris in possession of the field as leader. He could arrange publication
for the others or publish a magazine for them, he could
get them opportunities to speak, he could provide them

chances to earn a living. He could edit textbooks. He was a captain of industry in the field of culture, a Connecticut Yankee at the court of reason.

Most important of the things that Harris did was to keep the community stirred up over philosophy. He was a leader in the Philosophical Society which was founded in 1866 and an important member of the other philosophical and literary groups that sprang up in the city. We have seen how he affected Miss Blow. He had the same influence over many others. His religious conviction coupled with his usually clear exposition moved them to a passionate acceptance of his philosophy. Like Susan Blow these followers stood on the delectable mountains and beheld the Eternal City. Some of them were undoubtedly moved far beyond their capacity to understand clearly but that did not interfere with their ecstasy. Furthermore, he led in the interpretation of all educational problems in terms of the philosophy of Hegel.

The key to Harris' educational theory was self-estrangement.[10] The overcoming of self-estrangement by a later synthesis which picked up the primitive self and sublated it was only further emphasis on getting away from the isolated self. Education was for him in the first instance, "mediation," that is to say, it was the process of connecting the self with a larger whole, a beginning of self-estrangement. The first requirement of education was accordingly subordinating "likes and dislikes" to a "rational object."[11] To carry out this plan he insisted on discipline. "Corporal punishment was to be administered

10 Cf. W. T. Harris, "Science of Education," *Jour. of Spec. Phil.*, Vol. XIII, p. 205; also an "Analysis and Commentary" to accompany a paraphrase of Rosenkranz's "Pedagogics as a System" which appeared in Vol. XII.

11 *Ibid.*, p. 211.

by means of the rod." [12]   He would keep the kindergarten from getting disorderly through too great stress on freedom. He would not allow kindergarten methods to invade the primary grades. Nor would he let the methods of the primary grades regiment the kindergarten. The psychology of the growing child he believed, required a proper correlation of method and age.[13] Teachers and administrators were urged to keep grammar and mental arithmetic in their curricula until they could find something better. In the same spirit of discipline he would not allow the elective system to enter the colleges indiscriminately. Choice should not be given to students of insufficient maturity, and the new system should not be allowed to push the classics and mathematics out of the requirements for the Bachelor of Arts degree.[14] Instead of interpreting the higher aspects of life in terms of the lower he would interpret the lower in terms of the higher,[15] and thus keep up a certain moral tension. In the effort to impose organization on the educational process he used Hegelian terminology freely. In handling the subject of the education of women, for instance, he brought in the familiar triad of the Family, Civil society, and the State.[16] In considering moral education he referred to Chinese, Greek, and Roman civilization almost in the words of Hegel's *Philosophy of History*.[17]

All of this organization headed up for Harris in the absolute. The whole process "is the education of the hu-

---

12 *Ibid.*, p. 213.

13 *Cf.* his paper on "Kindergarten Methods, etc." *National Education Association Proceedings*, 1888, p. 448.

14 *Ibid.*, pp. 276-277.

15 *Cf.* his essay, "Biological Analogies in Educational Subjects," *National Education Association Proceedings*, 1902, pp. 220-221.

16 In his *19th Annual Report to the Board of Directors of the St. Louis Public Schools*, pp. 112-120.

17 In his *17th Annual Report, etc.*, p. 22.

man race by Divine providence." [18]   In writing on Negro education he said "Divine decrees broke up the eternal sabbath of blessed perfection, and created finite, imperfect beings, in order, it would seem, that there should be occasion for the exercise of this missionary spirit of divine charity." [19]   And the object toward which the divine was leading the race was a complete rationality and consequent freedom. "Holiness," he said,[20] "means moral perfection, purity from irrational caprice and passions. The divine human is the absolute, conscious reason — like man's ideal of moral perfection and rationality." The end was religion and Harris like Hegel found this goal in the Christian faith.

The field of the kindergarten shows perhaps most plainly Harris' ideas regarding unity and organization in education. Miss Blow states in her memorial address that Harris grounded the kindergarten in Eternal Reality and that those who entered the kindergarten work experienced a "sacred fellowship." Harris says that the Gifts and Occupations helped the child in the conquest of nature and the plays and games offered him in symbolic form the treasures of the experience of the race.[21] The child, he says, "ascends (through plays and games) from the world of nature to the world of humanity: from the world of things to the world of self-activity; from the material and earthly to the spiritual." The child attains a consciousness of "a higher self acting within his particular self." "Here (in songs and pantomimes) the child climbs up

---

18 W. T. Harris, "Science of Education," *Jour. of Spec. Phil.,* Vol. XIII, p. 208.

19 W. T. Harris, "Education of the Negro," *Atlantic,* Vol. LXIX, p. 722.

20 "Need of Moral Training," *Journal of Education,* Vol. XXVII, p. 131.

21 *Cf.* his "Kindergarten Methods, etc.," *National Education Association Proceedings,* 1889, p. 452.

through his symbolic pathway, through play, to the absolute mind." [22] The stress on symbolism by Harris was an emphasis on the connectedness and oneness of the universe, for if there were no unity symbolism would break down. Miss Blow writing in the spirit of Harris quotes part of a motto for the mother in one of Froebel's games:

"Whatever singly thou hast played
May in one charming whole be made."

The emphasis on symbolism brought in the resort to great art among the kindergartners. It is probably owing to Harris' influence through the kindergarten that Miss Blow wrote upon Dante. This brings us to Harris' general insistence upon the study of masterpieces.

A profound literary interest and activity marked the St. Louis Movement. Brokmeyer wrote his letters on Goethe's *Faust* which were published in early volumes of the *Journal of Speculative Philosophy*. Snider recounts how Mary E. Beedy, a teacher in the high school, first formed a private class in Dante and wrote an essay on the poet which he heard her read to some friends in the early seventies.[23] He tells also of an essay written by Mrs. Rebecca N. Hazard which was published under the title, "A View of Dante." L. F. Soldan is credited by the same writer with having written and lectured on the author of the *Divine Comedy*. Thomas Davidson, though at first condemning the Italian poet, took him up with enthusiasm after sojourning for a time in Italy. And later Snider himself lectured and wrote extensively on what he called the "Four Literary Bibles": Homer, Dante, Shakespeare, and Goethe. In all this Harris was a stimu-

---

22 *Ibid.*, p. 451.
23 D. J. Snider, *op. cit.*, p. 467.

lating influence. He urged in national associations that teachers' meetings be held to discuss the problems of the great works of literature and art.[24] He condemned Herbert Spencer for ignoring such subjects in his discussions of education.[25] In this connection it should be said that Harris' book on *The Spiritual Sense of Dante's Divina Commedia* is still regarded as an authority.

We may now ask what was Harris' concern with literature? Though it is not fair to characterize him as merely using literature to illustrate philosophical conclusions it must be said that his appreciation was largely controlled by his interest in the philosophical world-view and the attendant religious implications. He says in his work on Dante that "neither philosophy as such nor allegory can be the best feature of a genuine poet," but he thinks, nevertheless, that certain great poems show "the operation of a supreme principle." [26] In another connection he states that the educative function of the tragic and the comic consists in making us "conscious of the eternal elements of human nature — the divine human in some contrast with the finite and transitory." [27] Snider [28] thinks that Dante brought Harris back to his church. Thus literature like the other phases of Harris' work so far discussed brought out the organization side of the universe.

Literature stood close to another interest, that of art. Miss Beeson says in one of her letters to the writer of the

---

24 *Cf.* his contribution to *National Education Association Proceedings,* 1889, p. 314.

25 In his discussion, "Herbert Spencer," *National Education Association Proceedings,* 1904, pp. 219-220.

26 W. T. Harris, *The Spiritual Sense of Dante's Divina Commedia,* p. 2.

27 W. T. Harris, "Educational Value of the Tragic vs. the Comic," *National Education Association Proceedings,* 1898, p. 403.

28 *Cf. op. cit.,* pp. 471-472.

present paper that Emerson once said to Harris, "I wish I could see in pictures what you do." Though it would not be fair to say that all Harris saw in a picture was philosophy and religion, this appreciation also was definitely informed by philosophical and religious principles. In discussing the relation of art to religion he says, "Art is the piety of the senses, Religion the piety of the Heart, and Philosophy the piety of the Intellect." [29] Again in the same article he states that "art makes the invisible visible." [30] And further, "From the lowest spheres up, there is an increase of adequateness on the part of art to present the content of Religion." [31] In a Concord lecture on "Landscape Painting" given in 1882 he speaks of art as a means of attaining the infinite.[32] In the lecture he makes much of symbolism as the means of reaching this goal.[33] In Raphael's "Transfiguration" he finds antithesis and organic unity much in the Hegelian spirit. In the same spirit he finds in it sense, understanding, and reason. But he thinks the picture is romantic and aspiring and not finally satisfying.[34] In Michel Angelo's "Last Judgment" on the contrary he finds a painting that goes beyond the romantic to the repose of the eternal.[35] In art as in literature he finds the supreme value to be in an apprehension of the infinite.

All this interest in philosophy, education, art, and lit-

---

29 W. T. Harris, "Relation of Art to Religion," *Jour. of Spec. Phil.,* Vol. X, p. 207.

30 *Ibid.,* p. 204.

31 *Ibid.,* p. 209.

32 W. T. Harris, "Landscape Painting," *Concord Lectures on Philosophy,* 1882 (outlines), p. 136. (Pub. by Moses King, Cambridge, Mass., 1883.)

33 *Ibid.,* p. 138.

34 W. T. Harris, "Raphael's Transfiguration," *Jour. of Spec. Phil.,* Vol. I, pp. 53-57.

35 W. T. Harris, "Michel Angelo's Last Judgment," *Jour. of Spec. Phil.,* Vol. III, pp. 73, 77, 86.

erature was not limited to St. Louis. Even before the dispersion of which I shall speak later the St. Louis Movement was carried beyond the confines of the city. First there were other cities and schools where independent philosophical and cultural movements had been started which had friendly stimulating relations with Harris and other members of the group. There were, for instance, the coteries centering around Hiram K. Jones, the Platonist of Jacksonville, Illinois; Thomas M. Johnson, another Platonist, of Osceola, Missouri; William A. Jones, President of the Terre Haute Normal College; Samuel Emery, of Quincy, Illinois, and many other circles who received help from the St. Louis group. In addition a positive influence was flowing out of St. Louis as Harris traveled around making speeches on philosophical and educational subjects. At the height of the interest a halo centering in St. Louis included many hundred miles of surrounding country.

During these years the members of the St. Louis Movement, mainly under the influence of Harris, were living in a garden of Eden with only an occasional dissentient note to emphasize the prevailing harmony. The morning stars were singing together and rich bird notes sounded over paradise.

But an inner dialectic was working. Miss Susan Beeson in one of her last letters wrote of the "many years of successful efforts before the serpent crept in." I would have traveled far to learn about that "serpent." But the good lady died shortly after writing, and her revelations were never completed. The term may have had immediate reference to a rupture of relations between kindergarten leaders but in a broader sense the "serpent" that destroyed the cultural Eden of St. Louis was the principle of self-activity.

Harris himself had long been emphasizing this principle as inherent in idealism as such and as opposed by every type of naturalism. His own ingenious turn of mind, which had put a list of contrivances to his credit that would have done honor to a professional inventor, doubtless made him appreciate further the self-activity principle. One of his counts against Herbert Spencer was that his philosophy of education did not contain self-activity.[36] In his annual reports to the Board of Directors of the St. Louis Public Schools he repeatedly stressed this principle. In 1869 he emphasized the value of cultivating industrial talents. In 1870 he thought that self-activity and prescription must go together.[37] In the latter year he thought self-activity the reconciliation of radicalism and conservatism.[38] In 1871 he connected self-activity with our national idea of freedom.[39] Later he connected it with the industrial system. In criticizing Edward Bellamy's *Looking Backward* he made a strong argument for competition.[40] In an article on "Statistics of Socialism" [41] he characterized capitalism as self-activity. With this characterization in view, when the question of administering our island possessions came up in the later nineties, he stated his belief that whole nations should be apprenticed to industrial civilization even if we had to enforce it by military means.[42]

Outside of the St. Louis group self-activity dissociated

---

36 *Cf.* his paper on "Herbert Spencer," *National Education Association Proceedings,* 1904, p. 215.

37 W. T. Harris, *16th Annual Report, etc.,* p. 179.

38 *Ibid.,* p. 181.

39 *Cf.* his *23rd Annual Report, etc.,* p. 75.

40 *Cf.* his article, "Edward Bellamy's Vision," *Forum,* Vol. VIII, pp. 199 ff.

41 Published in *Forum,* Vol. XXIV, pp. 186 ff.

42 *Cf.* his "Educational Policy for our New Possessions," *National Education Association Proceedings,* 1899, p. 72.

from any rational control was by now overwhelming the
land like a cloud of locusts desecrating and destroying
everything in its path.   The city of St. Louis itself according to Snider was under a great economic illusion.   Everyone was "self-active," everyone believed that wealth was
to be rained upon him out of heaven, if he would only
assert himself.   Over the nation at large the same influence was abroad.   Railroads were being developed that
made Mississippi transportation look as archaic as an ox
team.   A city was growing at the foot of Lake Michigan
that had all the advantages of innumerable railroads from
the West and water and rail transportation to the eastern
coast.   The distinctive cultures that had begun to spot
the country in towns like Jacksonville (Illinois), Quincy
(Illinois), and Osceola (Missouri) were beginning to
crumble into the universal tide. Men of talent were hastening
to the new cosmopolitan centers of activity.   St. Louis,
in spite of its size and greatly to its surprise, found
itself to be one of those dissolving social entities.
In 1870 it thought it was ahead of Chicago in population,
but the census of 1880 put Chicago 150,000 ahead.   The
democratic-naturalistic flood after a brief up-surge of
idealism resumed its leveling course.

Inside the movement were numerous signs of that same
self-activity.   Brokmeyer had never been in sympathy
with the ecstatic mood of some of the members and would
upon occasion break forth into profane and titanic fury.
The standing disagreement between Harris and Davidson
has already been noted.   Snider, after putting several years
into the study of Hegel's *Logic,* went his own way into
Hellenism and general literature.   Though always rever-
encing Harris as a leader, he insisted on developing his

own talents in his own way. The estrangement between Snider and Susan Blow was probably a reflection of the difference of outlook that had been growing between Snider and Harris.

Further evidence of the same thing was the dispersion that began to take place about 1880. That was the year that Harris resigned the superintendency of the St. Louis Public Schools and moved to Concord, Massachusetts, to take charge of the summer school of philosophy that Alcott and Emerson had started. Brokmeyer went into politics and later found satisfaction among the Indians of Indian Territory. Though Snider alone of all the more active men in the original movement always came back to St. Louis, he went to Concord to lecture at the invitation of Harris, and also lectured in Washington and Baltimore.[43] Davidson went to England, later established a workers' College in New York, and after holding a school of philosophy for a brief time at Farmington, Connecticut, started conducting his famous summer gathering at Glenmore in the Adirondacks. Harris, Davidson, and Snider participated together in the literary schools that Snider carried on in Chicago for ten years. Howison went much earlier to the Massachusetts Institute of Technology and later built up his famous department of philosophy at California. Finally Harris was appointed United States Commissioner of Education. It will thus be seen that the St. Louis Movement in Philosophy was scattering to the four winds.

But something even more significant was happening in the line of self-activity. The names of James and Dewey were being heard in the land. James lectured on psychology at Concord, and the names of James and Dewey ap-

---

[43] *Cf.* D. J. Snider, *op. cit.*, p. 444.

peared in the *Journal of Speculative Philosophy*. The latter wrote at that time almost with the exact words of Hegel but his appearance was significant in the light of his later development. Here was soon to be little respect for the absolute and much contempt for the formal symbolism of Froebel. Here was coming in a rampant disbelief in *a priori* principles. The true was to become, in terms of one of these thinkers, the expedient. Mind was soon to be a stream of consciousness. Thinking, instead of being the independent arbiter of fate if not fate itself, was to be a means of survival and the attainment of satisfactions. Its concepts were to be characterized as having "cash value." The blind will was to be made the high authority back of belief. And soon the strenuous effort of Harris to induct the child into the traditions and institutions of his race was to be supplanted by a child-centered purposive activity. Following these teachings came other teachings whose dominant tendency was to deny still further that the world is one and to split it into many. Whatever one thinks of these doctrines it must be admitted that the democratic-naturalistic social process was continuing its leveling course.

What fortune befell the leaders of the St. Louis Movement in their scattering? Each was a coördinating center in his own situation, but the system he created soon began to sink to the general level. Harris occupied the United States Commissioner's office with great distinction for seventeen years. Then came a succession of successful politicians in that office. Brokmeyer died convinced that America was not yet ready for philosophy. Davidson returned to America to pass his influence on mainly through personal contacts. Snider after several years in Chicago came back to St. Louis where he opened his classes again in his old age. Howison's spirit doubtless goes marching on at California but it has failed to overcome the enveloping sordidness of the State. These men played their part well. They only suffered a universal fate.

As we contemplate the change in philosophic outlook from the days of William Torrey Harris and his friends we are likely to say with Matthew Arnold:

"The Sea of Faith
    Was once, too, at the full, and round earth's shore
    Lay like the folds of a bright girdle furled.
    But now I only hear
    Its melancholy, long, withdrawing roar,
    Retreating to the breath
    Of the night-wind, down the vast edges drear
    And naked shingles of the world.

". . . the world, which seems
    To lie before us like a land of dreams,
    So various, so beautiful, so new,
    Hath really neither joy, nor love, nor light,
    Nor certitude, nor peace, nor help for pain;
    And we are here as on a darkling plain
    Swept with confused alarms of struggle and flight,
    Where ignorant armies clash by night."

In the introduction to his *Spiritual Sense of Dante's Divina Commedia* Harris rejoiced that hell was simply a part of the divine dispensation — that is to say, punishment was in relation to sin. One wonders now if there is not a deeper more ontological dialectic than Hegel's needed to understand the world. Feeling that mankind lives on a thinner crust than formerly suggests such a conclusion. Perhaps there may be a deeper hell than Dante's, where unreason and utter madness rule, where punishment is not proportional to sin. By the same reasoning it may be possible that there is a higher reach of heaven than the *primum mobile*. All degrees of integration and disintegration may be possible and synthesis, instead of being the special favorite of God, may have only a fighting chance to exist somewhere in the infinite scale.

It is not desirable to go back to the cosmic subjectivism of Hegel. But under new conditions we can avail ourselves of many of the qualities and profound insights of Harris and his colleagues in the St. Louis Movement. We need Harris' passionate faith in the supremacy of reason, his belief in the symbolic connectedness of all parts of the universe. We need his sturdy defense of the individual and yet at the same time his insistence that the individual should do his distinctive part as a member of the infinite whole. We need his persistent application of philosophy to life in every phase and, with his philosophy, his organizing power. William Torrey Harris' life and works are a precious inheritance to which the American people in crises like the present can profitably appeal.

HARRIS AND THE JOURNAL OF SPECULATIVE PHILOSOPHY

BY EDWARD L. SCHAUB

It was in 1857 that William Torrey Harris, then a young man of twenty-two, moved from the East to become a teacher of shorthand in St. Louis and shortly thereafter an instructor in the public schools of that city. Seven and one-half years later, after having served as the Principal in one of these schools, he assumed the responsibilities of Assistant Superintendent. Within two years he then became Superintendent of Public Schools, an office which he filled for twelve years and which he relinquished only to return to the East, there to participate in the founding and in the brief life of the Concord School of Philosophy.

Significant indeed was the career of Harris during the period of twenty-two years when he resided in St. Louis. Of this city he became the cultural primate, and such he continued to be until the time of his departure to Concord. Gifted as a teacher and skilled as an administrator, rarely endowed with intellectual acumen and possessed of perspective, he contributed notably to those interests which a public school system is designed to foster. His promotions and his long service in the highest civic position of this system are a testimony not of political alliances but of educational power and success. Indicative of his efficiency in practice, as also of the scope and clarity of his intellectual outlook, is the system of cataloguing which he devised for the Public School Library and which, after its adoption in St. Louis, was utilized, in its entirety or in significant features, by other important libraries of the country. Characteristic of its author is the hope ex-

pressed by him, when including in the *Journal* [1] his scheme
of library classification, that his results "may prove useful not only to librarians, but especially to philosophical
students who desire to look over the whole range of human intelligence as realized in books." So solid were his
achievements and so illuminating his outlook as recorded
in his annual reports as Superintendent of the Public
Schools of St. Louis, that even from distant France he
received the honorary titles of "Officer of the Academy"
and "Officer of Public Instruction."

Possessed of zeal along with intellect, a missionary as
well as scholar, Harris extended his intellectual influence
far beyond the confines of school walls. He directed private classes devoting themselves to an understanding of
Kant and Hegel, of Dante, and of Goethe. More significant
still was his participation in the life of the St. Louis Philosophical Society. Though not the real originator of this
group, he was its "active organizer." [2] Not unnaturally
he became its first secretary, and, together with Brokmeyer, he remained what Snider describes as "in essence
the Society." [3] That this Society bore rich fruitage none
will dispute who are conversant with the history of St.
Louis, of the Concord School of Philosophy, or of the
Chicago Literary Schools.

Thus great being the contributions of Harris to the
public school interests and to the intellectual life expressed
and promoted by the St. Louis Philosophical Society, it
may indeed seem a hazardous assertion to range coördi-
nately with them his services in connection with the *Jour-*

---

[1] *Cf.* Vol. IV, pp. 114-29.

[2] *Cf.* Denton J. Snider, *The St. Louis Movement in Philosophy, Literature, Education, Psychology, with Chapters of Autobiography*, p. 7.

[3] *Ibid.*

nal of Speculative Philosophy. Yet there is much that may be advanced in support of such an evaluation, provided, of course, one may be allowed to sunder the journalistic enterprise from the Society whose organ, as well as that of Harris' own mind, it to a large extent initially was, and from the St. Louis Movement in general, of which in some broad sense the *Journal of Speculative Philosophy* was the intellectual offspring and vehicle.

Be it remembered that the first issue of the *Journal* appeared in January, 1867, a year that antedates the founding of any other definitely and significantly philosophical periodical in the English language.[4]   Subsequently the *Journal* was issued regularly, as a quarterly, for twenty-one years, and it terminated only with the twenty-second volume, two of whose numbers bear the dates of January and April, 1888, the third that of September, 1892, and the fourth that of December, 1893.[4a]   The *Journal* gave an opportunity for expression — indeed, in numerous cases stimulation thereto — to many vigorous minds, some of whom were just beginning to rise above the philosophical horizon: to Thomas Davidson, John Dewey, George S.

---

[4] Numerous other periodicals bordering on philosophy and making sallies into its field there, of course, had been. This indeed is obvious from the very conditions that impelled Harris to his venture. (See below.) A partial list of publications of this sort is furnished by Clarence L. F. Gohdes on page 14 of his volume, *The Periodicals of American Transcendentalism.*

[4a] With reference to certain incidental matters connected with the *Journal* we would note that its first fourteen volumes were edited in St. Louis, the succeeding seven volumes in Concord, and only the last volume in Washington, where Harris served at the time as the United States Commissioner of Education. The first thirteen volumes were printed in St. Louis, three different firms having a part in the task; the last nine volumes bear the imprint of D. Appleton Company, New York. In general we may say that the condition of the type used, as well as the carefulness of the typography and the accuracy of the proof-reading, are in conformity with the excellence of the subject matter. The quality of the paper used was at first not all that might be desired, but later it was improved. The double-columned page in which the *Journal* first appeared was abandoned with the third volume, and the type was then enlarged as a needed concession to the eye. Throughout, however, the material continued to be arranged very compactly, so that the twenty-two volumes of the *Journal* have less blank space than is to be found in other

Fullerton, G. Stanley Hall, G. H. Howison, William James, George S. Morris, Charles Peirce, and Josiah Royce, not to mention other Americans who likewise came to achieve distinction, such as Nicholas Murray Butler and Simon N. Patten; also to Canadians: S. W. Dyde and John Watson; and likewise to Europeans, of whom one might mention Edward Caird, Simon S. Laurie, J. H. Stirling, as well as W. Lutoslawski, whose brief article "On the Difference between Knowledge and Belief as to the Immortality of the Soul" was the last of the many carried by the eighty-eight numbers of the *Journal*.   Thus did the *Journal* act as a ferment within the philosophical life of America, as it further did through the encouragement and presentation of translations into English of much significant material from the classical thinkers.   It stirred thoughtful Americans generally to a rethinking of current logical, metaphysical, and religious doctrines; and it placed before them a reasoned organismic philosophy in obvious contrast with the various individualisms rooted in the life and prevalent in the teachings of the time.   The influence of the

---

periodicals.   In bulk the volumes vary somewhat. Beginning with volume nine the size of the separate numbers was increased from ninety-six to one hundred eleven pages each, though volumes fourteen and twenty-one are exceptional in that they contain a total not of four hundred forty-four but of four hundred fifty-six and four hundred fifty-two pages respectively. With the exception of volume seven, three of whose issues number their pages from one to ninety-six and one from one to ninety-two, all volumes number consecutively the pages of the four issues comprised therein. Save for volume four, the first five volumes each carry a table of contents which includes in alphabetical order the titles of all the articles previously published in the *Journal*; in the case of all the other volumes, the table of contents is restricted to the articles published in the four numbers of each; volume ten, however, includes in addition a general index, arranged alphabetically, of all the titles of the contents of all ten volumes, and volume fifteen prints, in addition, a complete index, ordered alphabetically, of all subjects together with all contributors given space in volumes one to fifteen inclusive of the *Journal*. Curiously variable, however, is the organization of the tables of contents. Though the *Journal* began with its sixth volume quite regularly to devote a certain amount of space to book notices (of which previously only a few had appeared in volume two), and beginning with the numbers of its tenth volume to include lists of books received, the tables of contents do not invariably include these headings, and when they do, their places within the tables vary in almost every conceivable manner.

Journal, moreover, spread far beyond the borders of the United States. Perry, indeed, makes the statement that the *Journal* "was better known in Europe than in the United States."[5] Affording some support to such a contention is the fact that the number of letters and contributions which European scholars submitted to the *Journal* is strikingly large when one considers the conditions of the time. It is facts such as these which compel us, when considering Harris' career, to give more than a merely subordinate place to his connection with the *Journal of Speculative Philosophy.*

That Harris continued as the sole editor of the *Journal* throughout its history, that he included in its pages much of his own best philosophical work,[6] and that he made substantial financial contributions to its support,[7] are easily established facts. Not so clear is the question as to the origin of the periodical. Some there are, as Townsend tells us,[8] who give the credit for the establishment of the *Journal* to Brokmeyer. Yet the justice of so doing seems at the very least to be doubtful. Some light on this matter is thrown by Stratton. At one of the meetings of the St. Louis Philosophical Society, he reports: "Harris said: 'We are going to have a German philosophical magazine.' Howison, surprised, asked who was to give the money for printing it. Harris replied: 'We don't propose to print it. We are going to make the papers and read them here, and put them away in the tin box.' Into the tin box, then, were

---

[5] *Cf.* Charles M. Perry, *The St. Louis Movement in Philosophy,* p. 67.

[6] Interesting in this connection is the following judgment of Snider's (*loc. cit.,* p. 100): "Harris, though philosopher, was deeply and essentially the journalist . . . his spiritual unit was the magazine article, not the organic book, which is or ought to be something generically other than a mere collection of periodical writings."

[7] *Cf.* Charles M. Perry, *loc. cit.,* p. 66.

[8] In his *Philosophical Ideas in the United States,* p. 117.

poured not only Harris's first papers, later published as
his *Contributions to Philosophy,* but also the papers by
him and others which grew into the periodical, so honor-
able a pioneer in its field, *The Journal of Speculative Philosophy.*"[9]   Denton J. Snider, who in 1866 and for years
thereafter was identified with the St. Louis Movement and
was closely associated with both Brokmeyer and Harris,
not merely refers to Harris as the founder of the *Journal*[10]
but in connection with his account of how he himself
brought out his many volumes through his own publishing
company, writes as follows: "Herein [*i.e.* in respect to self-
publication] I deem Harris the forerunner and the early
daring protagonist, when he started the *Journal of Speculative Philosophy,* in 1867, to publish his own work rejected
in the East. I remember it as one of his supreme moments
when I saw him bring down his clenched fist before a
group of his friends, affirming with vehemence: 'Now I
am going to start a Journal myself.' That was the primal
creative act of self-publication in the St. Louis Movement
years before my first dash in the same direction." [11] That
the volcanic Brokmeyer may previously have thrown out
some suggestion respecting the establishment of a philosophical journal may, to be sure, perhaps have been the
case. What seems clear, however, is that prior to the inci-
dent reported by Snider any such suggestion remained
lifeless. Moreover, it was Harris who at any rate developed and executed the plans embodied in the *Journal.* Some
indication of the absoluteness of his editorial control over
the enterprise from its very inception may be found in
the fact that the *Journal,* despite its settled policy of bring-

---

9 John   Wright   Buckham   and   George   Malcolm   Stratton,   *George
Holmes Howison: Philosopher and Teacher,* p. 50.
10 *Cf.* Denton J. Snider, *loc. cit.,* p. 96.
11 *Ibid.,* p. 480.

ing out English translations of the philosophical masters and especially of German idealists, never published Brokmeyer's translation of Hegel's *Logic*.[12]

In the case of a man like Harris the motivations to important action are not to be found in more or less accidental incidents or in dim impulse, but rather in clearly envisaged purposes. What really led to the founding of the *Journal* were reflections with respect to certain basic needs of American culture, and to the ways in which these might best be met. These needs were in the main determinative also of the character of the periodical, of its objectives, its scope, and its policies.

What were these needs as Harris saw them? They were threefold: religious, political, and intellectual. Examination of these various needs, however, and of the way in which they might most effectively be met, disclosed the fact that they indicated a single requisite as primary and as basic: that, namely, of a more adequate philosophical orientation and a more profound philosophical understanding.

In the sphere of religion, sheer traditionalism, though still enthroned, was nevertheless being subjected to severe assaults. These came from the side of a militant atheism or of an agnosticism which attacked the ideology and the central tenets of orthodoxy. In its defence of the latter, traditional religion found allies in groups of intuitionists, romanticists and mystics—allies, however, who ignored all the historical considerations so precious to traditionalism, and who, moreover, failed to give to religious dogmas either intellectual clarification or philosophical justification.

---

12 In speaking of this "perplexing omission" Snider (*ibid.*, p. 100) tells of Harris' "neglect, indeed his refusal to publish in his Journal, when he had space and means, the original source and first inspiration of the St. Louis Philosophical Society, namely, Brockmeyer's translation of Hegel's Logic."

To Harris it seemed clear that the call of religon was for philosophical support against its assailants. Moreover, religion as an experience of rational beings can, as it seemed to Harris, achieve the perfection and completion toward which it reaches out by its own nature only by acquiring a clearer self-consciousness of its essential reasonableness. "No truly religious man," he maintained, "would admit that his religion contained aught but the absolute truth. This absolute truth, embodied in such a form as to be *lived and felt* as religion, should also be *thought* as pure truth. The Piety of the Heart leads its possessor to renounce whatever comes between him and the divine mission of his life; the Piety of the Intellect leads to the renunciation of mere opinions, the delusions of the senses— to a seeking, through a speculative insight, the Truth which burns with a consuming fire the shreds of abstraction and stands before the soul in wholeness and holiness."[13] Thus, then, the *Journal* was motivated in part by the needs of religion, and these it kept in view to the end. The very first article in the *Journal* concludes with the sentence, "This is the *aperçu* of Immortality";[14] the last article published by it relates to the immortality of the soul and it closes with the contention that "the only way to bring more harmony between human actions and the teachings of religion is to associate religion with philosophy and undertake to prove, without any other authority than reason, what is assumed or believed on various historical authorities."[15] The words are Lutoslawski's but the thought they express was in the mind of Harris when he founded the *Journal,* and it entered into his purposes throughout the subsequent

---

13 *Jour. of Spec. Phil.,* Vol. II, p. vi.
14 Vol. I, p. 6.
15 Vol. XXII, pp. 440 f.

years. The first number of the *Journal* carried a translation from Schopenhauer entitled "A Dialogue on Immortality," and very shortly it presented a bit of Schopenhauer's *Ueber den Willen in der Natur* under the caption
"Schopenhauer's Doctrine of the Will."   The themes of
human freedom and immortality, as well as that of theism,
thenceforth recur with frequency. Blocked off at the head
of the cover page of every issue of the *Journal* beginning
with the third number of volume fourteen are the familiar
words of Novalis: "Philosophy can bake no bread; but
she can procure for us God, Freedom, and Immortality."

But, as we have said, Harris was prompted by political
and social, as well as by religious, needs. The former no
less than the latter, he believed, were such as could be met
only by a changed philosophic outlook and sound philosophic thought. In his word "To the Reader" with which
he opened the first number of the *Journal,* and thus shortly
after the close of the Civil War, Harris expressed himself
as follows: "The idea underlying our form of government
had hitherto developed only one of its essential phases—
that of brittle individualism—in which national unity
seemed an external mechanism, soon to be entirely dis-
pensed with, and the enterprise of the private man or of
the corporation substituted for it. Now we have arrived
at the consciousness of the other essential phase, and each
individual recognizes his substantial side to be the State
as such. The freedom of the citizen does not consist in
the mere Arbitrary, but in the realization of the rational
conviction which finds expression in established law. That
this new phase of national life demands to be digested and
comprehended, is a further occasion for the cultivation of
the Speculative."[16] That such considerations entered deep-

---

[16] *Jour. of Spec. Phil.,* Vol. I, p. 1.

ly and continuously into Harris' purposes is indicated likewise by words printed a year later. Writes Harris: "One
may mistake the men filling the offices of the state for the
state itself, and hold likely enough that the state is a very
unimportant affair; forgetting meanwhile that in our modern state very little of its essence is embodied in the officers
who have the name of administering it, but that its essence
is all the more embodied in the individuals who constitute
society, so that little is left for the external visible government to do. But were the organism of the state removed—
whose essential function is to secure to each man the frui-
tion of his deed, good or bad—the individual deprived thus
of the organism which elevated him to such importance as
individual, would shrivel up into an atom so insignificant
that life would not be worth the having." [17]

Deeply impressed as he was with the needs of religion
and of politics, Harris felt even more imperatively those
connected with science and the ideational life generally.
These also, he was convinced, could be satisfied only by
speculative philosophy. Flowing at the time were strong
tides of naturalism and materialism, stirred by such as
were overawed by the success of current science and by
the works of Spencer, Darwin, and Huxley. These tides
needed to be stemmed. Moreover there was a growing
number of people eager to acquire the satisfactions which
philosophy affords.[18] Furthermore, science itself, as it
seemed to Harris, had reached a crisis. Against the various attempts in the early part of the century to portray
physical nature speculatively and metaphysically, science
had reacted with such violence as to embog itself in a

---

17 *Ibid.*, Vol. II, p. vi.
18 It was for them that Harris wrote the series of six articles entitled
"Introduction to Philosophy" which began in the first issue of the *Journal*.

swamp of dense facts. As Harris put it in a phraseology reminiscent of Hegel, science had rejected pure thought in favor of a "sensuous knowing" which, "rests on mere isolated facts of experience; accepts the first phase of things, or that which comes directly before it, and hence may be termed the stage of *immediateness*." The result was "crude, undigested masses all co-ordinated; each . . . [being] in and for itself, and perfectly valid without the others."[19] Inevitably, however, thought began its work not merely of testing and relating but, more especially, of discovering dependencies. It learned, as Harris stated it, that "the first phase of objects is phenomenal, and depends upon somewhat lying beyond it."[20] As the culmination of the earlier stage came attempts, such as Humboldt's *Cosmos,* to put results into encyclopedic form, and further to investigate such subjects as matter and masses. But then reflection entered, and with it came an investigation of functions and a recognition of the abstract category of force; and, writes Harris, "straightway we are in the second stage. Matter, as such, loses its interest, and 'correlation of forces' absorbs all attention." [21] Now it was this second stage, as Harris interpreted the thought of the time, that the great body of contemporary scientists had reached. Its ablest exponent he saw in Herbert Spencer. Since the point of view is one that transcends the immediacy of "sensuous knowing" and "denies truth to the immediate," Harris spoke of it as the stage of *mediation.* To show its self-contradictory and self-nugatory character, and thus to lead thought on from the stage of the understanding and reflection to that of speculation

19 *Jour. of Spec. Phil.,* Vol. I, p. 8.
20 *Ibid.*
21 *Ibid.,* p. 9.

at which reason "considers a phenomenon in its totality, and thus seizes it in its *noumenon*" [22]—such was one of Harris' chief concerns in the establishment and in the conduct of his *Journal*. Writes Snider:[23] "The first essay of his own I ever heard Harris read was a refutation of the philosophy of Herbert Spencer, whose works were then in the process of publication and discussion over the country. Thus it may be said that Spencer gave the primal impact which pushed into print the St. Louis Journal of Speculative Philosophy by way of opposition." This essay it was with which Harris opened the first issue of the *Journal* after addressing a preliminary word "To the Reader" and explaining in a brief article what he understood by "The Speculative."

Thus, as Harris looked upon the contemporary world of religion, politics, and science, its greatest desideratum was a more active preoccupation with philosophy, and this, he believed, could be brought about with peculiar effectiveness by a journal. Now, Harris had already become convinced that there is one form of philosophy, and one alone, which is essentially sound and which was therefore fit to meet the needs of the day. Hence his inclusion of the term "speculative" in the name which he gave to the *Journal*. The meaning which he attached to the term has already been adumbrated. More definitely we might say that for Harris speculation and speculative philosophy meant a transcending of simple and sheer empiricism to an apprehension in which particulars are construed as indissoluble from universals, the finite from the infinite; a transcending also of the view that things, while to be sure not existing isolatedly and not knowable immediately through sense, are

---

22 *Ibid.*, p. 8.
23 *Loc. cit.*, p. 118.

yet fully intelligible through processes, called reflection or understanding, which disclose the relationship of things with one another—a transcending, we say, of this view to one which realizes that things must be recognized as possessing self-identity, and that the organ of genuine comprehension is therefore the concrete universal. It meant a transcending of the standpoint from which identity and distinction, immediacy and mediacy, are irreconcilable contradictories to one which permits a recognition of their inseparability, a recognition which implies that the ultimate principle of intelligibility is that of self-relation, such as we find exemplified, in its most complete expression, in self-consciousness and self-determination. Thus speculative philosophy meant to Harris a metaphysical as contrasted with a positivistic doctrine; and a metaphysics which declares that the acquisition of truth is within the power of intelligence, that reality is comprehensible, and which therefore proceeds to invade and to place under the mastery of reason that territory which Kant, Hamilton, and Spencer had declared unknowable. Such conquest, however, requires a procedure quite other than those describable by the principles either of inductive or formal logic. "To detect a speculative system," writes Harris, "ask the following questions of it: (1.) 'Is the highest principle regarded as a fixed, abstract, and rigid one, or as a concrete and self-moving one?' (2.) 'Is the starting point of the system regarded as the highest principle, and the onward movement of the same merely a result deduced analytically; or is the beginning treated as the most abstract and deficient, while the final result is the basis of all?' In other words, 'Is the system a descent from the first principle or an ascent to one?' This will detect a defect of the method, while the former question, (1,) will detect defects in the content or subject matter of the system."[24]

In genuine speculation, Harris contended, form and content are organic to each other; the method is inseparable from the substance of the doctrine. Truth is objective, and this it can be only if thought follows the requirements of the objects with which it is engaged. To approach a body of material with a set of concepts found significant in other fields, or to deal with it through the use of methods appropriate elsewhere cannot but preclude the possibility of a rationally satisfactory knowledge; to expound philosophical ideas in terms that are non-speculative is to abandon all prospect of communicating their essential meaning. Understanding, thus, involves an identification of thought with reality. This is true no matter what may be the object of rational concern. Philosophical systems, thus, must likewise be approached in this manner; a realization of their nature affords at once a positive appreciation of their significance and a realization of the point at which they fail to include that which they themselves imply and which alone can give them solidity and completion. That system of philosophy must be valid which is implied by all others and which itself harbors no negative, in that it includes within itself all antinomies and all that any of its constituent elements require for their stability, so that in it thought finds its complete expression and satisfaction. Such a system Harris believed was put forth, at least in its general pattern, by Hegel.

Some there were in Harris' day who proclaimed the need of an American philosophy. Harris, however, was of the opinion that what the United States most required was not American thought but American thinkers. And for

---

24 *Jour. of Spec. Phil.,* Vol. II, p. 2.

the development of real thinkers he considered nothing superior to preoccupation with mankind's master minds. Significantly creative achievements in the realm of philosophy, he was convinced, may be expected only of such as have captured the vision and have comprehended the doctrines of the great speculative philosophers, of whom there were many from Plato and Aristotle down, but of whom the most mature were the German idealists, especially Hegel. To present liberal portions of their work in English translation, and thus to make their thought widely available, Harris devoted a large fraction of his *Journal* from its very first number to its last; and many other pages he used for translations of essays in which leading French and German thinkers dealt with speculative philosophers, as well as with other geniuses who portrayed the real and vouchsafed the truth through the medium of the pictorial and the literary arts, as did, for example, Da Vinci, Beethoven and Goethe. Even the most casual survey of the *Journal* cannot but bring to one's attention two further facts respecting its contents, namely the very meager consideration given to the dogmas that distinguish the various historical religions of the world, on the one hand, and, on the other, the unusually large amount of space devoted to theories of art, to the nature of the various fine arts, and to discussions of particular works of art, whether in the form of music, poetry, painting or sculpture. For this, too, Harris had his reasons. In substance, though not in form, the message of real art, as of religion, he was convinced, is identical with that of sound philosophy. This message, however, is under certain circumstances conveyed by art with an effectiveness peculiar to itself. Speaking of art, Harris said: "Its sensuous content acts most readily upon the incipient phases of culture, and its higher forms work with a genial effect in developing the spiritual faculties. Art is moreover a subject for free reflection, while Religion has not as yet become such among us. The constraint prevailing in the latter province seriously hinders the pure thinking that is requisite to see the speculative depth of the great ideas that underlie the religion of the day, while those who break away from the popular forms fall into an abyss of nullification such as unfits them for sound positive insight."[25]

In general it must be admitted that the literary and the typographical styles characteristic of the *Journal* are not distinguished. This, also, was recognized by Harris himself. In referring to the matter, however, he gives not excuses but reasons. Let us note them. He says: "In order to secure against ambiguity, it is sometimes necessary to make inelegant repetitions, and, to give to a limiting clause its proper degree of subordination, such devices as parentheses, dashes, etc., have to be used to such a degree as to disfigure the page. Capitals and italics are also used without stint to mark important words. The adjective has frequently to be used substantively, and, if rare, this use is marked by commencing it with a capital."[26] Those articles in the *Journal* which present translations of Fichte, Schelling, and Hegel will perhaps not be severely criticized for their deficiencies in the way of literary elegance and clarity save by those who have never themselves sought thus to transcribe the works of these philosophers. In the case of the original articles, however, a stouter defence is needed. This can best be supplied by reference to the writers' conception as to the nature and the proper method

---

25 *Ibid.*, Vol. II, p. v.
26 *Ibid.*, Vol. I, p. 128.

of genuinely philosophical thought. To the mind of most of the *Journal's* contributors philosophy does not represent a superficial and inaccurate rehearsal of the general findings of science and history, nor a mere stringing together or external synthesis thereof. It possesses a standpoint altogether its own, and a method and content peculiar to itself. Hence its terminology and its mode of expression must be unique if they are to be appropriate. Where, as in the case of philosophy, the form is organic to the content and the method is inseparable from the subject matter, the linguistic expression can be faithful and intelligible only if it is rigorously dominated by the requirements of philosophy itself instead of being attuned to the familiarities of the non-philosophical.[27] Concessions to the latter can but obscure and thus render unintelligible, rather than intelligible, the philosophical ideas which the writer aims to communicate. Really to open the field of philosophy to all one must present philosophy itself. The use of non-philosophical modes of expression, however, can but bar the gates of philosophy while yet deluding readers into the belief that they are being guided within its realm. Thus, one cannot but expect that philosophical conceptions and the course of reasoning essential to them will seem dismally dark to such as have not ascended to a plane of reason which transcends not merely sense and picture thinking but likewise abstract reflection, in order, through the medium of concrete universals, to afford rational insight and

---

[27] Thus, writes Harris in beginning a series of articles designed as "a course of discipline for those who are beginning the study of philosophy": "Strictly *popular*, in the sense the word is used—*i.e.*, signifying that which holds fast to the ordinary consciousness of men, and does not take flights beyond—I am well aware, no philosophy can be. The nearest approach to it that can be made, consists in starting from the common external views, and drawing them into the speculative, step by step." (*Jour. of Spec. Phil.*, Vol. I, pp. 57 f.)

comprehension. To Harris and his associates their procedure meant not the adoption of some philosophical esotericism from which some are excluded either arbitrarily or by choice; it meant the procedure characteristic of all distinctively philosophic thought.[28] The comprehension thereof, they realized, was indeed an arduous matter and many there doubtless would be who would fail to achieve it—many others, also, who would make no serious effort in that direction and for whom philosophical converse could therefore be but as gibbering voices in the blackness of night.

To some minds only simple straightforward sentences are intelligible; others are not rebuffed by longer linguistic structures of a conditional and hypothetical nature. But in neither of these ways, as Harris thought, could philosophical ideas be expressed. "There are three styles," he contended, "which correspond to the three grades of intellectual culture. The sensuous stage uses simple, categorical sentences, and relates facts, while the reflective stage uses hypothetical ones, and marks relations between one fact and another; it introduces antithesis. The stage of the Reason uses the disjunctive sentence, and makes an assertion exhaustive by comprehending in it a multitude of interdependencies and exclusions. Thus it happens that the style of Hegel is very difficult to master, and cannot be translated adequately into the sensuous style, although many have tried it. A person is very apt to blame the style of a deep thinker when he encounters him for the first time. It requires an "expert swimmer" to follow the discourse,

---

28 *Cf.* Hegel's statement: "Only what is perfectly determinate in form is at the same time exoteric, comprehensible, and capable of being learned and possessed by everybody. Intelligibility is the form in which science is offered to everyone, and is the open road to it made plain for us all." (Preface to *Phenomenology of Mind, Hegel Selections* edited by J. Loewenberg, p. 11.)

but for no other reason than that the mind has not acquired the strength requisite to grasp in one thought a wide extent of conceptions."[29]

There is doubtless much in and about the *Journal of Speculative Philosophy* which must today impress us as eccentric and antiquated. Nevertheless, when we consider its nature as a whole and the influences it exerted, we may well hesitate before pronouncing extravagant Townsend's estimate of it as "probably more significant in the annals of American philosophy than any other publication."[30] This journal, be it remembered in simple justice, was in a unique degree the creation of W. T. Harris.

---

[29] *Jour. of Spec. Phil.*, Vol. I, p. 128.
[30] Harvey Gates Townsend, *loc. cit.*, p. 120.

THE POLITICAL PHILOSOPHY OF HEGEL IN
A FRONTIER SOCIETY

BY HARVEY GATES TOWNSEND

The leading conscious historian of the St. Louis Movement in philosophy[1] has unconsciously used a phrase in
characterizing his own zeal for publication which applies
to the whole movement with a somewhat surprising accuracy. He says that he was moved by a relentless desire for
"self-publication." The student of this small chapter in our
intellectual history will hardly fail to observe the ironic
fitness of the phrase. By this statement I do not mean to
imply that the leaders of the St. Louis Movement can be
accused of petty vanity nor of indulging in some disgust-
ing program of exploitation of themselves for personal
gain. Far from it! They were rather, one and all, carried
along as on a flood tide of unselfish devotion to an idea.
What I mean is that the key to their logical, their metaphysical, and their political philosophy is the key of the
inner dialectic of the psychological self.

It is seldom possible to date a so-called "movement,"
whether philosophical or otherwise, with such satisfying
accuracy as we are able to date this one. It began in 1858
with the meeting of Harris and Brokmeyer, and virtually
ended as a distinctive group of men and ideas some twenty
years later when Harris began to turn his eyes and his
steps back to the New England whence he came. The *Journal of Speculative Philosophy* lingered on in an intermittent
way for another decade and a half but before it ceased
publication in 1893 it had lost the single-minded, almost

---

[1] Denton J. Snider, *The St. Louis Movement, etc.* Sigma Publishing Company, St. Louis, 1920.

missionary quality with which it had begun in 1867 and
continued for ten or fifteen years. The two decades from
1858 to 1878 were filled with the turmoil of the American
civil war. In a political, though not in a military sense,
Missouri was at the center of the storm and St. Louis was
at the center of Missouri.

In 1857, the year in which Harris arrived there, St.
Louis was the epitome of American frontier civilization.
It was the chief gateway to the west and northwest and
without a rival as the supply base of unnumbered explora-
tory expeditions and land settlement migrations so elo-
quently recorded by historians like Turner. Though by
no means a large city in sheer number of residents (in
1840, the population of St. Louis, excluding St. Louis
county, was 16,469; in 1850, 77,860; and in 1860, 160,773),
it was nevertheless the metropolis of an empire so vast as
to fill the mind with fantastic dreams. Out yonder lay
virgin plains of untold fertility, mountains of gold and
precious stones to be had by the rugged, self-reliant pros-
pector. Men who returned from California and Pikes Peak
could remember most vividly the very features of the new
lands beyond the horizon of which the as yet uninitiated
eager young adventurers most wished to hear. Why talk of
dry deserts and burning sands, of exposure, deprivation
and despair when there were so many more interesting
topics of conversation? The imagination expanded in this
atmosphere to an incredible degree. To "go west" was the
vernacular for escaping evils of all sorts and descriptions.

The St. Louis movement in philosophy is the natural
child of German romantic literature and American romantic politics. On the side of German romanticism its ancestry
is already well established. Indeed, so great an emphasis
has been laid on this aspect that the other has been neg-

lected. The *Journal of Speculative Philosophy,* the major
record of the "school," has an academical sound and a very
distinctly academical flavor. Its editor was a schoolmaster
who subsequently occupied an official position as United
States Commissioner of Education and thus established his
association in the annals of American history with things
scholastic. The magazine itself is full to the brim with an
esoteric doctrine greatly removed from the dusty Oregon
Trail, with its covered wagons and freight trains, bor-
dered by the bleaching bones of men and animals. In it
there is no reference to gold rushes, to Mormon prophets
and scandals, to land agents and railroads, to mules and
vigilance committees. The Hegelian philosophy was a po-
tent prophylactic. As compared with his successors in the
office of Commissioner, Harris was pedantic. It is a marvel
to the present generation of public school teachers that he
was able to give currency to his abstruse phrases and his
fine-spun doctrines. Though there was little or no conscious
effort to exclude the ruck and circumstance of the common
life, Harris chose to move in the rarified atmosphere of
scholastic symbols because he was convinced by Brokmeyer
that the theoretical explanation of all these prodigious
events was found in the Hegelian law of dialectical growth.
He even followed Brokmeyer in subordinating the ethico-
political philosophy of the master to his more abstruse logic.
Expressing an opinion of the relative importance of the
works of Hegel, Harris lists the logic at the head, while
the ethical and political works are sixth and seventh in
the list of eight.[2]

Whatever significance such a judgment by Harris had
or has, it must not be allowed to obscure the larger fact
that there was an urgent social *milieu* in which the flint

----

2 *Cf. Jour. of Spec. Phil.,* Vol. III, p. v.

of Brokmeyer struck fire. A political refugee inspired by what he considered a gospel of social salvation, after the vicissitudes of random experience, was settled in the midst of the dramatic episodes of a struggle for national union. With his fellow countrymen he was predisposed to take the side of the Union against the forces of dissention and disruption. If he had had no previous acquaintance with the Hegelian philosophy, he could not have hit upon a solvent theory to bring order out of chaos or a systematic defense of his faith more to the point than Hegel's. But he was not unacquainted with Hegelian philosophy. Moreover, his acquaintance with it was not the acquaintance of a scholastic mind but of an ardent enthusiast for social betterment and a humanitarian Utopia. Though it would admittedly be difficult to establish from the pages of the *Journal* or other material expression of leaders of the St. Louis "school," it is nevertheless quite apparent to the student of the movement that its center of gravity was political rather than scholastic. They found in the German romantic philosophy a ready-made formula by which they could interpret the life of the frontier and the tragic conflict of civil war.

In 1860 one in every seven persons in the entire Missouri population was foreign born and one in fourteen was German born.[3] In St. Louis, the very center of the German colony, the proportion of German born residents was, of course, much greater. It is a matter of record that it was the Germans of St. Louis who took the initiative and sustained the effort to keep Missouri loyal to the Lincoln administration. It may seem paradoxical that the men of '48 fleeing from the Prussian tyranny should have made a bible of Hegel's *Logic*—the Hegel who has been called the one

---

[3] *Cf.* Lucien Carr, *Missouri*, p. 261.

to glorify the Prussian state. A study of this paradox, however, tends not only to reveal the inner significance of the St. Louis movement but incidentally to correct the popular estimate of Hegel.

The reputation which Hegel has with British and American students is too seldom based upon a genuine appreciation of the events within which and out of which his political philosophy arose. Though there is little time for a glance into the troubled waters of German politics in the time of Frederick William III, we should remember that Hegel's political writing from 1798 until the year of his death in 1831 must be seen against the background of a disunited, distracted and helpless Germany. At the beginning of this period there were literally hundreds of independent political and social jurisdictions in Germany.[4] The struggle to unite these warring petty states into a united nation was a terrific one and the task was accomplished in the end at the cost of much blood and of a mounting injustice. Hegel's continuous defense of the ideal of a united Germany, though modified with the changing years, was neither at the beginning nor at the end a philosophy of isolated and irresponsible central authority and power. It was rather a studiously acquired and, in its total form, a very technical philosophy of the progressive integration of wills through the unfolding of reason. The dominant organicism of his theory, suggesting the modern totalitarian state, was nevertheless combined with the doctrine of free participation by individuals and groups which should associate Hegel unmistakably with the then rising tide of revolutionary liberalism. His unhappy praise of the Prussian state, if taken in abstraction, does indeed lend itself to the theory of absolutism in politics, but it is not

---

4 *Cf.* E. F. Henderson, *A Short History of Germany,* Vol. II, p. 219.

to be taken in abstraction. It was his unfortunate formal expression of a political synthesis which is significant only if taken in living connection with the thesis and antithesis of his ubiquitous dialectical triad. In the second division of his philosophy of spirit "abstract right" is set over against an equally "abstract morality" and the two are fused in the culminating doctrine of the "ethical state."

In attempting a compliment to Hegel's wisdom, Treitschke unwittingly reveals his own misconstruction of Hegel and also lays bare what is probably the common source of a widely prevalent misinterpretation of Hegel's political theory. Says Treitschke, "A sounder view than that of most of his contemporaries was taken by young Hegel concerning the situation of the empire. He saw in this chaos 'the juxtaposition of two contradictions, that a state is at the same time to be and not to be', and he found the ultimate cause of the trouble in the vaunted German freedom." [5] Treitschke confuses the first moment of the Hegelian dialectic with the *de facto* cause of an historical situation. It would be more correct to say that Hegel found the *beginning* of the trouble in the vaunted German freedom. But even that statement, if the word *beginning* is allowed to carry its usual connotation of temporal priority, is misleading. What Hegel meant is that the abstract claim of freedom by an individual or a subordinate group within the social organism is the prime logical aspect of a concrete social process. Treitschke misses the meaning of Hegel, a meaning more adequately expressed by von Sybel, who says, "The spirit of individualism had torn the empire into pieces. Only the further development of this very spirit in the special governments could produce a

---

[5] *History of Germany in the Nineteenth Century*, tr. by Eden and Cedar Paul, Vol. I, p. 225.

remedy." [6]　Hegel's argument was not directed against freedom but against an abstract freedom which professed to be the whole idea of the state. It is the "further development of this very spirit," to use von Sybel's words, which is the positive doctrine of the state in Hegel's political theory.

Bosanquet had a clear perception of the liberalism of Hegel. Commenting on a letter from the young Hegel to Schelling, Bosanquet says, it "is revolutionary and humanitarian throughout. We know, of course, how the opposite of all this was imputed to Hegel in his later years. Nevertheless, this is the real clue to the system." [7]　A French writer, in the course of a recent and valuable paper on Hegel's political philosophy, has rightly concluded, "Et Hegel d'ajouter que la puissance effective d'un Etat réside, non dans ses habitants ou ses guerriers, non dans la fertilité de son sol ou dans la grandeur de son territoire, mais uniquement dans *sa cohésion,* dans *l'union des parties avec le Tout national.* Cette simple remarque contient en germe toute la philosophie politique de Hegel." [8]

It was not uncommon for Hegel to appear in American literature of the mid-nineteenth centry as a political liberal. In a series of papers by Emilio Castelar in *Harper's New Monthly Magazine,* during the early seventies, entitled, "The Republican Movement in Europe," Hegel is represented as the most conspicuous of the liberals. The opening sentence of his ninth paper [9] is, "The true philosophy

6 Heinrich von Sybel, *The Founding of the German Empire,* tr. by M. C. Perrin, Vol. I, p. 14.

7 *Germany in the Nineteenth Century,* 2nd Series, Publications of the University of Manchester. Historical Series, Vol. XXIV, pp. 190-191.

8 E. Vermeil, *La pensée politique de Hegel,* in *Etudes sur Hegel,* p. 180. His italics.

9 *Harper's New Monthly Magazine,* Vol. XLVII, p. 578. According to the *Jour. of Spec. Phil.,* Vol. VII, No. 4, p. 88, probably some 500,000 persons read Harper's.

of progress is that of Hegel." "I know well," continues the author,[10] "how much can be said by those who judge systems by their isolated parts more than by their spirit and their totality. They will say that after having condemned the historical School, I place among the philosophies of progress the illustrious metaphysician of history. They will say that after having vindicated the liberty of thought, I praise the philosophy of the state, bound to the state and its interests. They will say that after having proposed to follow in all its spheres the German republican movement, I pause before the philosopher who declared monarchy an institution essential to human society, and who, dissolving the pure idea of right in the historical movement of this idea, at last justifies all institutions and sustains even the punishment of death. But I believe that a philosophy should not be judged by its fragments, its isolated parts, where evident contradictions may be found with its general sentiment and spirit." Admitting that Hegel surrendered to the power of monarchy the author nevertheless holds that the essence of Hegel's political theory is in his dictum that "The history of the world is the history of liberty."

In the *Journal of Speculative Philosophy* itself a similar contention shines through at various places. In Volume VI, a translation of Rosenkranz's *Hegel as Publicist*, presents Hegel as the defender of a state produced by the exercise of rational freedom. It was Hegel's drastic criticism of the radical "Student Corps" which gave him a reputation for anti-democracy. Says Rosenkranz,[11] "Hegel had great horror of a state founded merely upon right, where only the externality of personal justification made the frigidity of egoistic rectitude a dominant prin-

10 P. 579.
11 *Jour. of Spec. Phil.*, Vol. VI, p. 270.

ciple . . . this standpoint of abstract internality he
treats with almost malicious disparagement." Again, "But
all the blame which can be attached to Hegel's construction
arises from the profound idea which he had formed of
the state, in which he saw the realization of ethics." [12]

By and large, this was the estimate of Hegel's political
philosophy held by the leaders of the St. Louis movement.
To them, for whatever reasons, Hegel was the prophet of
a reunited state after the tragic "dialectic" of civil war.
To them the southern position was that of "abstract right,"
the northern position that of an equally "abstract morality,"
and the United States that was to be was identified with the
synthetic "ethical state." Faithful to the letter and also to
the spirit of their master, they did not shrink from the conflict but went to meet it in the settled conviction that no
real synthesis in history arises except through the tragic
process of the dialectic of events.

It is quite evident that the St. Louis movement in philosophy was formed in the furnace of military and political circumstance, under the inspiration of Brokmeyer.
Throughout the record there sounds the rumble of the
Hegelian *triadic movement*. These men who were held together by the passionate Brokmeyer busied themselves
applying the fixed formula of Hegel to each new development or phase of the gigantic struggle. Thus Fort Sump-
ter is the "thesis"; Camp Jackson, the "antithesis"; and the
declaration of war the "synthesis." Or again, the St. Louis
"illusion" (*i.e.,* the real estate boom), the "thesis"; the
founding of the Philosophical Club, the "antithesis"; and
the building of the Eads bridge, the "synthesis." When
they saw the rival city of Chicago begin to flourish it was
the "antithesis" of St. Louis. And they hailed the great

---

12 *Jour. of Spec. Phil.,* Vol. VI, p. 275.

fire as the end of that "phase," hoping it would be followed by the revived St. Louis as the ultimately established "synthesis." In Vol. II, p. 128, of the *Journal*, Anna C. Brackett enshrines the dogma in verse:

"For only where the one is twain,
And where the two are one again,
Will truth no more be sought in vain."

These random examples of the naive expression of the discovery of an Hegelian dialectic in the stirring events of a frontier civilization in the midst of a struggle for national union are nevertheless of large interpretative significance.

Harris's Hegelianism was largely formed before he read the *Logic*. It is of interest to notice that although he met Brokmeyer in 1858, it was not until after the close of the war that he read the *Logic*. Yet in 1867-9 he was publishing an *Introduction to Philosophy* in the *Journal* which follows Hegel so closely as to be virtually a paraphrase.[13] We must suppose that until after the war his acquaintance with Hegel was chiefly mediated by the turgid mind of Brokmeyer, filled as it was to overflowing with the oracular political philosophy of Hegel. At the end of Volume I, of the *Journal*, Harris reviews Paul Janet's work, *Essai sur la dialectique dans Platon et dans Hegel*. In this review he reveals a comprehension of Hegel's meaning and a critical ability greater than he showed when he came to publish his book on *Hegel's Logic* in 1890. In his *Introduction to Philosophy,* he saw Hegel's *Phänomenologie des Geistes* in its proper setting as propaedeutic to the system and as the anatomy and physiology of the human spirit— the dialectic of the self.

I do not, of course, mean to imply that Harris had gone

---

13 See especially Vol. II, pp. 177 ff.

astray in his opinion that the *Logic* is the core of Hegel's philosophy. On the contrary, that judgment can be substantially defended, and it was Brokmeyer's judgment. What I do intend to say is that Harris got his insight into Hegel under the inspiration of Brokmeyer in the tumultuous decade—1858 to 1867. His later writing on Hegel shows less unity and security of vision as time goes on. Whether it was because of a greater independence of his master or because of the intrusion of rival dogma can hardly be determined; but in either case the natural result was the development of Harris's own mind.

In the autobiographical notes in the preface of his *Hegel's Logic* Harris says,[14] "In 1866 I for the first time read through Hegel's larger logic, reading it in the English translation that had been made for myself and two other friends (George Stedman and J. H. Watters), by Henry C. Brockmeyer, in 1859 and 1860. I copied the work entire from the manuscript and am sure I read every word of it. But I am equally sure that I did not understand at the most any thing beyond the first part of the first volume, and could not follow any of the discussions in the second and third volumes, or even remember the words from one page to another. It was all over my head, so to speak. I had of course made myself acquainted with the categories and sub-categories of the work years before through histories of philosophy, and was gradually learning to think something into them; but I could make little of Hegel's deductions or discussions of them."

Perhaps the most significant quotation, however, is in the succeeding paragraph where we read, "Mr. Brockmeyer's deep insights and his poetic power of setting them forth with symbols and imagery furnished me and my friends

---

14 P. xii.

of those early years all of our outside stimulus in the study of German philosophy. He impressed us with the practicality of philosophy, inasmuch as he could flash into the questions of the day, or even into the questions of the moment, the highest insight of philosophy and solve their problems. . . . We studied the 'dialectic' of politics and political parties and understood how measures and men might be combined by its light." [15] Surely this is abundant testimony for the substantial truth of my thesis that it was the solvent power of the political philosophy of Hegel which enabled it to strike so deep a root into the cultural soil of a frontier civilization.

These early American expounders of Hegel found his "dialectic" the key to unlock the mysteries of the immediate drama of history. The instrument of interpretation was the unfolding experiences of the individual self. They found reason in the civil strife because they interpreted political events as episodes in the predestined development of the ethical state through the triadic movement of affirmation—negation—reconciliation.

Such at least was the Hegelianism of the St. Louis days of the "movement." When Harris finally faced the problem of expounding Hegel in a more technical manner in his book, *Hegel's Logic,* in 1890, he had gotten away from the social and political origins of the movement. His later interpretation is not only a more abstruse but a less adequate one

There is reason to suppose that Harris's later Hegelianism was modified by two forces. The first of these was his native New England transcendentalism. He was a *bona fide* Yankee. He grew up in an atmosphere of missionary zeal and throughout his life his industrious devo-

---

15 *Ibid.,* p. xiii.

tion to good causes was of a passionate and religious sort. His determination to serve mankind carried him to triumph as a school man and really lay at the basis of his quixotic venture in the Concord School of Philosophy. By it he hoped to spread the true gospel. He admired Emerson greatly and even Alcott seemed an oracle to him. His controversy with Davidson had driven him to defend Hegel against the charge of pantheism. Davidson's philosophy would save the individual and leaned strongly toward empiricism and pluralism. Harris was put upon the defensive and became labored in his effort to make Hegel square with the rising empiricism and pragmatism of the day.

The second force to modify his early understanding of Hegel's philosophy was his reading of Oriental literature. Speaking significantly of this in his *Hegel's Logic,* he says,[16] "As early as 1856 I had begun to read Oriental literature, but had not seized its essential spirit." Fifteen years later he thought he had discovered the agreement between Hegel and "Hindoo thought." And finally he testifies that about 1885 he "began to see that Hegel himself has not deduced the logical consequences of his system in the matter of the relation of nature to the absolute idea." [17]

It has often been pointed out that New England transcendentalism had little resemblance to its German original in Kant. Hegelianism at St. Louis was also different from the German original. It flourished partly because on its political side it was appropriate to the occasion. The leaders of the movement correctly saw in Hegel a liberal philosophy of progress and a doctrine of triumphant political union. This was enough to give it root and to make it an important element in our cultural history.

---

16 Preface, p. xiii.
17 *Ibid.,* p. xiv.

HARRIS AND INDIAN PHILOSOPHY

BY KURT F. LEIDECKER

Indian philosophy is today still a concept that must be referred to almost apologetically. Various circumstances are responsible for this attitude, but the *causa materialis* remains, as a hundred years ago, language. The more remarkable it is that William Torrey Harris (1835-1909) provided a large space for the treatment of Indian philosophy in his principal sketch of the history of thought.[1] This is surely to the credit of the astuteness and foresight of this great philosopher.

Not all is Hegelian echo.[2] The most valuable of Harris' contributions are the results of his own researches in the best translations available to him at the time. These include Colebrooke's translation of the Sānkhya Kārikā, which he borrowed from Ralph Waldo Emerson, Wilkins' and Thompson's translations of the Bhagavad Gītā and Wilson's translation of the Viṣṇu Purāṇa. Further information on Indian philosophy he gleaned from *The Dial, The Massachusetts Quarterly* and the works of Cousin, Sir William Jones, Max Müller and Rhys Davids. More remotely he learned of Indian thought through Emerson, Thoreau, Babu Dwijendra Nath Tagore, P. C. Mozoomdar, John J. Elmendorf, Edwin Arnold, Charles D. B. Mills, John Davies, Laura E. Poor, William Cunningham and others.

---

[1] See the *Jour. of Spec. Phil.*, Vol. X, (1876), pp. 231-237. Quoted below as *Outline*.

[2] Harris' indebtedness to Hegel is sufficiently known and therefore does not require comment here.

Our source-material for Harris' treatment of Indian thought is not confined to his philosophical articles, numerous though they are. We are as liable as not to find him discussing Vedāntic or Buddhistic concepts in an article on kindergarten methods as in a government report.[3] Acquaintance with Indian thought coincides with the first serious study of Hegel, about 1858, or even with the reading of Emerson's "Brahma," which appeared in 1857. Familiarity dates from 1861.[4] In his book on *Hegel's Logic,* however, he tells us that he began reading Oriental literature as early as 1856.[5] His attitude may be characterized as cosmopolitan in interest, uncompromisingly American and Christian in point of view.

Harris was not unaware that Orientalism would be a perpetual lure and gain in volume as it becomes better known. Did not Goethe, Emerson and a hundred lesser lights condone, yes capitulate to views seemingly the antithesis of the spirit of industry and democracy? By Orientalism is meant not the civilization of the Chinese or Japanese, nor that of the Persians, but that of the Hindus whom Harris called "the most remarkable, purely Oriental people." [6]

Indian philosophic thought was regarded by Harris as a necessary stage in the development of mind.[7] Sanskrit literature holds the "embryonic shapes and metamorphoses of modern literature." It is "a kind of pre-historic

---

3 *Cf.* Henry Ridgely Evans, "Complete List of Writings of W. T. Harris, Chronologically arranged with Subject Index," in *Report of the Commissioner of Education for the year ending June* 30, 1907, Vol. I (Washington, 1908). Published also separately.

4 *Books That Have Helped Me* (N. Y. 1888), p. 23. First published in *Forum,* April, 1887.

5 *Hegel's Logic* (Chicago, 1890), p. xiii.

6 *Cf. The Philosophic Aspects of History* (1890).

7 *Cf. Jour. of Spec. Phil.,* Vol. XIV, p. 238.

adumbration of European thought." [8] Again, he called it precocious wisdom.[9]

Every student of Indian philosophy will thank Harris for saying that Oriental thinking is not merely theological. He criticized Hegel and his followers for having fallen prey to the error of relying mainly on missionary accounts and excluding the Orient from their histories of philosophy.[10] He himself derives philosophy and theology from Egypt, India, and Persia.[11] The New England transcendentalism he credits with pioneer work by drawing Asia into its perspectives.[12] In sociology and the history of philosophy, Oriental peoples should always be studied.[13]

Harris is ready to acknowledge the value of Hindu thought for Western culture, though he cannot see how we can ever recognize the validity of its fundamental ideas. He says: "Its value is chiefly negative, aiding us in getting rid of sensuous conceptions in the realm of thought. It is a sort of cathartic for the imagination." [14]

On the whole, Harris prefers to interpret Indian thought as nihilism, abstractionism and negative absolutism. Why he does this is obvious to anyone who realizes that pedagogy is the soul of Harris' speculations. A sharply drawn contrast with Western thought facilitates didactic exposition, and buttresses at the same time innate and traditional views. Harris was not quite oblivious to

---

8 *Outline;* also, *The Western,* Vol. I (n.s. 1875), p. 635.

9 In *The Western,* Vol III (n.s. 1877), p. 211. Unless otherwise stated, in references to *The Western* the n.s. is meant.

10 *Cf. Outline; Johnson's Universal Cyclopedia* (1898 *ed.*), Vol. VI, p. 576.

11 *Cf. The Western,* Vol. I, p. 635. Here the familiar *ab oriente lux!*

12 *Cf. A. Bronson Alcott, His Life and Philosophy* (Boston, 1893), Vol. II, p. 596.

13 *Cf. ibid.,* p. 664.

14 *Books That Have Helped Me,* p. 23.

the fact that he may have done violence to Indian philosophy in this sweeping interpretation.

He grants, for instance, that the Sāṅkhya, the Bhagavad Gītā and the Viṣṇu Purāṇa, perhaps somewhat abstractedly, give expression to a "truly spiritual theory," [15] and he expounds selected passages to that effect. If there is virtue in the Bhagavad Gītā—and Harris leaves no doubt in our mind that there is—he should have gone one step further and revamped his criticism of Hindu philosophy.

In the case of Indian philosophy, language has concealed more than it revealed. Harris had a little knowledge of Sanskrit,[16] but he did not have enough to allow him to penetrate philologically the spirit of the Hindu philosophers.

In his own words, language, as "spiritual protoplasm,"[17] opens the inner workings of the mind of the race.[18] Parenthetically he in one passage [19] remarks: "A philologist of insight would know when he saw the Greek language, and the form of its sentences, that there was a nation designed under Providence to solve the theoretical problem of the world." If this is true of Greek, it is true to an even higher degree of Sanskrit, and Harris contradicts himself when he implies that maturity of spiritual development does away with grammatical inflections.[20]

---

15 *The Western*, Vol. I, p. 647.

16 As proven by various philologic discussions turning around such words as *adhyātman, manvantara, mahātman, maharṣi, rajah,* and Punjab, as well as some interest in Indo-germanic origins.

17 *Lectures read before the American Institute of Instruction at Fabyan's, White Mountains, July* 8-11, 1879 (Boston, 1879), p. 105.

18 *Fifty-fourth Annual Meeting of the American Institute of Instruction. Lectures, Discussions, and Proceedings. White Mountains, July* 11-13, 1883 (Boston, 1884), pp. 150-151, *et al. loc.*

19 *Jour. of Spec. Phil.,* Vol. XV, p. 310.

20 Cf. *Lectures read, etc.* (1879), p. 108. Similarly, *U.S. Bureau of Education. Report of the Commissioner of Education for* 1893-4, pp. 624 f.

So much has been said about language, for together with a Christian outlook it forms the presupposition for the peculiarities we notice in Harris' interpretation of Indian philosophy. The theological preoccupation, moreover, explains why Harris favored the Sāṅkhya. Both it and Christianity have a basis in dualism, though the Sāṅkhyan dualism is a very subtle kind. And here we meet a strange phenomenon: Harris, who so keenly appreciated a Hegelian, Fichtean and Schellingean idealism never spoke appreciatively of the Hindu idealism in the Upanishads and Vedānta.

To be sure, he mentioned the Vedānta system [21] and Pūrva and Uttara Mīmāṁsās.[22] The Nyāya and Vaiśeṣika are also mentioned.[23] But that the pure idealism of the Vedānta was not discussed may be explained only in that he feared for the integrity of his dialectic system if he had to account properly for this type of Oriental philosophy. Staunchly he maintained his view of the irreconcilability of Orientalism and Occidentalism, pantheism and theism, tyranny and democracy. Never should the twain meet, except the East acknowledge defeat, the burden pass from the white man's shoulder and the eternal dialectic cease at least in its geographic phase.

The key-word to Harris' interpretation of Indian philosophy is "negative unity." He sought to cover the many-hued and verdant growth of Hindu speculation by a Hegelian term that would grant it a modicum of right to exist, but show at the same time its transitory character. The presupposition rests with both, Hegel and Harris, on

---

[21] *Cf. Psychologic Foundations of Education* (Vol. 37 of the *International Education Series*), New York, 1899, p. 217.

[22] *Outline.*

[23] There may not be more than half a dozen references to each in Harris' voluminous writings, if that many.

an *aperçu*. Today we know, of course, much more about
Indian philosophy than in Harris' days, and although East
and West still remain dialectic terms in *Weltanschauung,*
we have come to value more in the Orient than just a
negative phase.

Harris' picture of Indian thought is best traced from
pure speculation to attitude-formation and basis of Indic
civilization.

Metaphysical world-ground is *brahman* ("Brahm,"
"Brahma"). This *brahman* is defined variously as a unity
which is formless,[24] all-devouring and primordial,[25] abstract [26] and negative.[27] Finitude and imperfection are
utterly incompatible with *brahman;*[28] *brahman* is pure,
empty being or existence (not *an* existence),[29] an empty
absolute,[30] transcendent [31]—even with respect to consciousness. It is a first principle "so abstract that no predicates
except negative ones may be applied to it." [32] The Hindu's
idea of the divine "is defined as the negation, not only of
everything in nature, but also of everything human. Nothing that has form or shape or properties or qualities—noth-

24 *Cf. Books That Have Helped Me,* p. 23; *Jour. of Social Science,* No.
15 (1882), pp. 1 f.; *Jour. of Spec. Phil.,* Vol. XXI, p. 359; *Proceedings of the
13th Annual Meeting of the Lake Mohonk Conference of Friends of the Indian,*
1895, p. 38; *New England Jour. of Education,* Vol. LVII, p. 4. See also
Marietta Kies' *Selections from Harris' Writings* (N. Y., 1890), p. 240.

25 *Cf. Jour. of Social Science,* June 1885, p. 8.

26 *Cf. National Education Association, Journal of Proceedings and Addresses* (1889), p. 653; *The Chautauquan,* Vol. VI, p. 192b; *Psychologic
Foundations,* pp. 276, 360; *New England Jour. of Education,* Vol. LVII, p. 4.

27 *Cf. Jour. of Spec. Phil.,* Vol. I, p. 238 and Vol. XV, p. 416; *Psychologic Foundations,* p. 217.

28 *Cf. Fifty-fifth Annual Meeting of the American Institute of Instruction. Lectures, Discussions, and Proceedings* (Boston, 1884), p. 40; *Third
Yearbook of the National Herbart Society* (1897), p. 70.

29 *Cf. Jour. of Spec. Phil.,* Vol. I, p. 252; *Education,* Vol. XI, p. 267.

30 *Cf. The Philosophic Aspects of History; Jour. of Spec. Phil.,* Vol.
XV, p. 252.

31 *Cf. Jour. of Spec. Phil.,* Vol. XV, p. 208; *Education,* Vol. XI, p. 267;
Psychologic Foundations, p. 217. See also Kies' *Selections,* p. 240.

32 *The Philosophic Aspects of History.*

ing, in short, that can be distinguished from anything else can be divine . . . This is Pantheism. It worships a negative might which destroys everything." [33]

No attribute whatever attaches to *Brahman,* be it of quantity or quality, mode, self-hood, individuality or personality.[34] What remains is nothing, and the best way of thinking of *brahman* would be to think of nothing; [35] "pure naught or Brahm." [36]

Let these few selected blank imputations be enough for the present. A similar tirade of negatives any god of pantheism had to face. True, the Hindu does not endow his ultimate metaphysical principle with human foibles and nature's frailties; he says *neti, neti,* not this, not that, if you wish to define *brahman* by concepts taken from the phenomenal. But he also says with the Upanishads; *brahman sarvam idam, brahman* is this world-all, and, if fullness were taken from fullness, fullness would yet remain. *Brahmam purnam, brahman is the plenum.*

Amusing is a slip of Harris' pen when, in an early article,[37] he defined the absolute of pantheism, and hence also *brahman,* as pure thought. He carefully avoided it in his later writings. Instead, he committed a cardinal error by attributing to *brahman* unconsciousness, or lack of consciousness in any shape or form.[38] Throughout, this

---

33 *The Chautauquan,* Vol. VI, pp. 192 f. So also *National Education Association Proceedings,* 1889, p. 653; *Psychologic Foundations,* p. 360; *New England Jour. of Education,* Vol. LVII, p. 4.

34 *Cf.* in addition to the references in the preceding two notes: *Jour. of Social Science,* No. 15, pp. 1 f: No. 20, Pt. II, p. 8; *The Chautauquan,* Vol. VI, p. 438b; *Jour. of Spec. Phil.,* Vol. XXI, p. 359; *Hegel's Logic,* p. 125; *Education,* Vol. XI, pp. 267 f; *The Independent,* Vol. LV, p. 1842; *et al. loc.*

35 *Cf. The Western,* Vol. I, p. 644; *Poet-Lore,* Vol. I, pp. 255, 259; *Education,* Vol. XI, pp. 267, 268.

36 *Jour. of Spec. Phil.,* Vol. XV., p. 416.

37 *Cf. ibid.,* Vol. I, p. 252.

38 *Cf. ibid.,* Vol. XV, pp. 208-9, and Vol. XXI, p. 359; *Jour. Social Science,* No. 15, pp. 1 f, and No. 20, Pt. II, p. 8; *Education,* Vol. XI, pp. 267 f; *Lake Mohonk Conference,* p. 38.

thesis was maintained by Harris, and only once he qualified it by saying: "With varying degrees of consistency,
the religions of Central and Eastern Asia are pantheistic,
and hold the highest principle to be unconscious. . . ." [39]

No Hindu following any of the philosophical schools
will grant that his ultimate ground of existence is unconscious. He will assert the very opposite, that *brahman* is
consciousness *par excellence,* and he will discover this error
in Harris' definition of consciousness.

Harris makes consciousness contingent upon the existence of an object-subject relation. And since in *brahman*
there is avowedly no distinction whatever [40] he concludes
flawlessly that *brahman* is an unconscious entity.[41] Also
from another angle *brahman* to him must mean unconsciousness. Since consciousness is limited apparently to
and by a self, and *brahman* is infinite, the latter must also
lack consciousness.[42]

Really, a misunderstanding of Sanskrit terms lies at
the root of Harris' statement that it is an Oriental tenet
that consciousness is finitude.[43] A somewhat similar error
based on deficient translations made Schopenhauer recognize his blind will as a metaphysical principle in the Upanishads.

At least in one case we can definitely point to an er-
roneous interpretation of terms. Harris takes *ahaṁkāra*
to mean consciousness.[44] Now, *ahaṁkāra* is, literally, the

---

39 *North American Review,* Vol. CXXXI, p. 243. But *cf.* pp. 244 and 245.

40 "The absolute negative unity neither exists for anything else nor for
itself; it is utterly distinctionless. It is the same as pure nothingness."
Psychologic Foundations, p. 217. *Cf. The Western,* Vol. I, p. 640; *The Chautauquan,* Vol. III, p. 195; *et al. loc.*

41 *Cf.,* e.g., the discussion of the Sāṅkhya in *Educational Review,* Vol.
XXIX, pp. 27-29.

42 *Cf.,* e.g., *Psychologic Foundations,* p. 277.

43 *Cf. Jour. of Spec. Phil.,* Vol. I, p. 252; *The Western,* Vol. I, p. 647; etc.

44 In *Poet-Lore,* Vol. I, p. 254; *cf. Hegel's Logic,* pp. 173, 300.

"I-maker." It may never be translated by consciousness. Here, a complete view of Hindu philosophy must be called in for an understanding. As philosophic principle, *ahamkāra* is on a lower plane than consciousness, and is, indeed, the *principium individuationis* which, psychologically, is often interpreted as selfishness, and then associated with *abhimāna.* Nowhere is *ahamkāra* represented as an ultimate reality of the nature of *ātman* or *brahman.*

Furthermore, the Hindu will challenge that consciousness implies difference such as obtains in ordinary perception and reflection. The consciousness of *brahman* is a state of realization, *jñāna,* in which the *coincidentia oppositorum* has become a fact. It is described as *brahmānanda,* the bliss of *brahman.* And, surely, the Hindu who does not regard his *nyāya, jñāna-yoga, vijñāna* and *vidyā* as mental gymnastics but wishes to reproduce in himself *jñāna* and *ānanda,* does not prepare himself for emptiness or unconsciousness. Nowhere in philosophic literature is sleep or death counseled—which would be the nearest approach to what Harris considered the absolute in Indian philosophy to be.

Harris himself facilitates our understanding the *brahman* of the Hindus by pointing out parallels in the history of Western thought. Gnosticism and Neo-platonism are the "Western reflection" of the Oriental formless and void Absolute "at Alexandria." [45] Basilides and Valentinus, Proclus and Jamblichus have a supreme principle similar to *brahman;* so have the Cabala [46] and the Arabian philosophers.[47] Eleatic being is of a like nature.[48] Spinoza's

---

45 *Cf. Jour. of Spec. Phil.,* Vol. XXI, p. 359.

46 *Cf. Books That Have Helped Me,* p. 24.

47 *Cf. Jour. of Spec. Phil.,* Vol. IX, p. 327 and Vol. XI, p. 336; *Hegel's Logic,* p. 34.

48 *Cf. Psychologic Foundations,* p. 222.

substance is nothing but a negative unity.[49]　Carlyle lapses into Orientalism.[50]　Faust, as long as he was in the clutches of Mephistopheles was a pantheist.[51]　Alcott is Oriental.[52]　Polish thought tends toward an "Oriental unity which it feels as a deep sentiment inherited from a prehistoric life." [53]

Modern science and philosophy, in so far as they set up an unconscious source of the universe, are simply the "Avatara of pantheism under a new form," a "revival of Orientalism." [54]

But above all it was Emerson who boldly came forth with his poem "Brahma" which expresses the Hindu feeling in a modern and superbly artistic garb.　And it was this decided stand of this genius that tempered Harris' condemnation of the Oriental Absolute.　He admired Emerson, perhaps he even sought to emulate him as some are wont to believe.　By speaking of this poem frequently and citing it in whole or part [55] he did not wish to imply a criticism of Emerson's "compend of Oriental pantheism," but presented it as a prerogative of a poet who loathes the trivial life of mortals.　"Emerson kept this stalwart form of idealism as a sort of medicine which he

---

49 Cf. ibid. and p. 219; also The Life and Genius of Goethe, ed. F. B. Sanborn (Boston, 1886), p. 387; and Hegel's Logic, p. 72.

50 Cf. Books That Have Helped Me, p. 22.

51 Cf. The Life and Genius of Goethe, pp. 385 ff; Poet-Lore, Vol. I, pp. 401 ff; The Independent, Vol. XLIX, p. 1035.

52 Cf. A. Bronson Alcott, Vol. II, pp. 604 ff.

53 Jour. of Spec. Phil., Vol. IX, pp. 335 f.

54 National Education Assn. Proc., 1888, p. 443. In scientific pantheism, the problems lie somewhat different. But this is not the place to discuss Harris' views in the matter.

55 Cf. especially the article "Emerson's 'Brahma' and the 'Bhagavad Gita'," Poet-Lore, Vol. I, pp. 253 ff; also The Western, Vol. I, course of reading on pp. 578-586 and p. 654; Jour. of Spec. Phil., Vol. IX, p. 336 and Vol. XV, p. 416; The Genius and Character of Emerson, pp. 373-380; Hegel's Logic, p. 143; A. Bronson Alcott, Vol. II, pp. 607 f.; Educational Review, Vol. XXIX, p. 27.

could produce on occasions when confronted with the Gorgon of materialism in any new shape." [56]

Harris is essentially correct when he characterizes the Hindu view of creation as emanation. It is difficult, of course, to speak of a Hindu view when every conceivable philosophic position has been held by the Hindu thinkers. Yet, the solution of the problem of the One and the Many has been made basically in the manner of Hegelianism as a dialectic development rather than a genetic history. If you will, it is a development of negative, and back to positive unity.

With *brahman* defined as completely negative, Harris naturally encountered difficulties when he set out to convey a picture of the emanation of the world (the development of particularity) and reabsorption back into *brahman*.[57] From negative unity alone nothing is to be gained. Harris' Hegelian background would have placed not the least obstacles in the way of his understanding the Hindus on this point.[58] On the contrary, his equipment was singularly excellent.

Likewise, his Western realism and activism rebelled against the Hindu idea that this vari-colored life and world should be *māyā*. That *māyā* meant illusion could be brought in harmony with the conception of negative unity. We notice two exceptions that reveal an insight into the *Sāṅkhya*. These will be discussed below.

Several uses of *māyā* may be distinguished. Barring the metaphorical use, Harris described the product of *brahman's* creation or emanation, as *māyā*, a dream that

---

56 *A. Bronson Alcott,* Vol. II, p. 607.
57 *Cf.* especially *Jour. of Spec. Phil.,* Vol. I, p. 238; *Outline; The Chautauquan,* Vol. III, p. 195; *Psychologic Foundations,* p. 217.
58 *Cf.,* e.g., *Jour. of Spec. Phil.,* Vol. XVII, pp. 348 ff.

has no substance, no reality to it,[59] proceeding from nothingness and returning to nothingness.[60] The process of the formation of *māyā* is correctly interpreted as the appearance of distinction in the unity.[61] Yet, if we search for the *causa materialis* as well as *efficiens* it is again wrongly ascribed to the presence or awakening of consciousness. In carrying this thought to its logical conclusion, Harris ascribes to the Hindus the doctrine that consciousness is illusion.[62] Nothing could be farther from the truth, as we have seen.

An ulterior motive can easily be distinguished in this persistent assertion that *māyā* is plain illusion, and that the world is illusion, not mere phenomenon.[63] For, if *māyā* is the phenomenal—and contextual studies of Hindu sources render it more than probable—then it would fit perfectly into the Hegelian logic [64] but would be highly inconvenient not only in a history that unfolds itself in this manner but also for a positive conviction that Christianity and Western civilization are synonymous with progress and culture. This latter was, however, the soul and life-work of the mature Harris. Hence, Indian thought had to yield him the negative term in his dialectic.

Indeed, we must agree with Harris that if *māyā* is plain illusion, the study of nature, the inventorying of natural objects and science are vain undertakings,[65] and it might

---

59 *Cf. The Chautauquan,* Vol. VI, p. 193; *National Education Assn. Proc.,* 1889, p. 653; *Psychologic Foundations,* p. 360; *New England Jour. of Education,* Vol. LVII, p. 5; *et al. loc.*

60 *Cf. The Chautauquan,* Vol. III, p. 195.

61 *Cf. Educational Review,* Vol. XXIX, pp. 28 f., etc.

62 *Cf. The Philosophic Aspects of History.*

63 *Cf. Psychologic Foundations,* p. 217.

64 *Cf.* the very interesting passage on pp. 287-8 in Vol. III of *Jour. of Spec. Phil.*

65 *Cf. Fifty-fifth Annual Meeting,* p. 41; *Hegel's Logic,* p. 86; *The Philosophical Review,* Vol. III, p. 12; *Lake Mohonk Conference,* p. 38.

then be said *a priori* that the Orient could not have invented science.[66] The fact that the Occident has developed science is due, according to our author, to Christianity.[67] However, have we not in Sanskrit literature systematic treatises on medicine, husbandry, economics and many other aspects of *māyā,* and has not, in many cases, science advanced in the West in conflict with religion?

Similar negative consequences are in store for the individual in this illusory world headed for a negative unity. The *saṁsāra* problem has a very subordinate place in Harris' discussions of Hinduism. As a matter of fact, however, it occasioned a great part of Indian philosophy, and the relation of the individual soul to *brahman* is not an artless vanishing in *brahman.*

Harris himself subscribed to a view against which few Hindus would raise an objection. "The ego can abstract all else and yet abide—it is the *actus purus*—its negativity annulling all determinations and finitudes, while it is directed full on itself, and is in that very act complete self-recognition." [68] And, furthermore, the ego is "the undetermined possibility of all determinations. Since it is undetermined, it is negative to all special determinations. But this ego not only exists as subject, but also as object—a process of self-determination or self-negation. And this negation or particularization continually proceeds from one object to another, and remains conscious under the whole, not dying, as the mere animal does, in the transition from individual to individual. This is the *aperçu* of Immortality." [69]

Being involved in *saṁsāra* Harris explains, unphiloso-

---

66 *Cf. Education,* Vol. XI, p. 270.
67 *National Education Association Proceedings,* 1903, p. 356, *et al. loc.*
68 *Jour of Spec. Phil.,* Vol. I, p. 188.
69 *Ibid.,* p. 6.

phically, as "punishment for the exercise of appetites and
desires in the life on earth," [70] epistemologically, as the
result of domination by *māyā*.[71] Overcoming *māyā* is
equivalent to identification with *brahman*. When *māyā*,
the dream, fades away, all creatures vanish and hope for
individuality is forthwith abandoned.[72] But it is at this
juncture that Harris parts company with the Hindus. For,
union with a negative absolute destroys all individuality
whatever, while preservation of individuality is the supreme achievement of Christian thinking.

The *ātman-brahman* speculation, the dialectic of soul
and world-ground, is the heart of Indian philosophy. That
the solution of the problem of individuality must be a different one from that pictured by Harris, is evident from the
fact that *brahman* is not a negative unity, and *māyā* is not
illusion. If, then, for the Hindu, *brahman* is something
positive, a species of super-consciousness, the individual
ātman does not simply vanish; and if, moreover, *māyā* is
akin to the phenomenological in Hegel's sense, the *ātman*
attains its own by realizing itself apart from *māyā*. It is
in this way that *mokṣa*, salvation, is obtained.

Hence, *mokṣa* is not the destruction of individuality.[73]
The *ātman* is in all Indian philosophy a conscious entity,
and as such it is, with Hegel and Harris,[74] immortal, because it contains within itself its limits or determinations
and thus cannot, "like finite things, encounter dissolution
through external ones." For this reason the following interpretation cannot be maintained, namely, that if we ac-

---

70 *New England Jour. of Education*, Vol. XVI, p. 313.

71 *Cf. Outline.*

72 *Cf. New England Jour. of Education*, Vol. LVII, p. 5.

73 *Cf. The Western*, Vol. I, p. 642; *Jour. Soc. Sci.*, No. 15, pp. 1 f.; *The Chautauquan*, Vol VI, p. 193; *The Philosophic Aspects of History; Arena*, Vol. XVII, p. 354.

74 *Cf. Jour. of Spec. Phil.*, Vol. I, p. 62.

cept *brahman* we would only seem to be, "for when he looked at us and 'placed us under the form of Eternity' we should vanish." [75]

The true nature of the *ātman* is disclosed in self-knowledge, one of the cardinal methods in Indian philosophy, from the earliest Upanishads onward. Indeed, *brahman* is considered the universal *ātman,* and hence Harris' assertion [76] that *brahman* "cannot be a self, but on the contrary must be a self-less being," is wholly unfounded. We must, therefore, repudiate the statement that to the Hindu consciousness and self-knowledge are disease,[77] or that progress to the divine is decay.[78] Here again it is the misunderstanding of *ahaṁkāra* that is to be blamed.[79] The Brahman, like ourselves, renounces not selfhood, but selfishness.[80]

By far the most serious objection against Indian philosophy is that it fails to recognize the value of personality and neglects to ascribe it to *brahman.* This seems indisputable, inasmuch as *brahman* is the *tremendum* which is so overpowering that the individual dares not predicate human elements of it. Therefore, *brahman* is of neuter gender, and the pronoun commonly used for the highest being is usually *tat,* It. Still, it would be wrong to say that Indian philosophy, on the whole, has looked askance at any personal approach between the human and the divine. The Vedānta, not to speak of the Yoga, concedes that Indian philosophy, on the whole, has looked askance with the metaphysical world-ground is expedient. Shiva-

---

[75] *Ibid.,* p. 238.
[76] In *Education,* Vol. XI, p. 267.
[77] Cf. *Lake Mohonk Conference,* p. 37.
[78] Cf. *Jour. of Spec. Phil.,* Vol. XV, p. 209.
[79] See above.
[80] Cf. *Poet-Lore,* Vol. I, p. 257.

ism, Viṣṇuism and the whole of *bhakti*-worship presuppose a human bond with *īśvara* or *īśa,* the Lord, without sacrificing too much of its metaphysical aspects. If we yet take into account Tāntrik speculation with its feminine *śakti* ultimate, it would seem that God as person is not typically Christian, but Indian. The highest flights of speculation, however, made the ultimate something distinct and above the personal phase of manifestation.

Thus, not all of Hinduism is directly concerned in the charge that God, with the Orientals, is not only not personal, but inhuman,[81] and that in order to become like him we would have to get rid of our humanity.[82] The high esteem in which a wise man is held, the sincere though often misguided devotion to the person of a Brahman, and finally the Buddha-ideal according to which each one may attain enlightenment—these surely testify to a thoroughgoing humanism and the proximity of the human and the divine.

Various are the consequences which flow from Harris' interpretation of *brahman* and *māyā.*

Grace, Harris concludes, cannot be exercised by *brahman.*[83] Yet, the doctrine of grace is found already in the Kaṭha and Śvetāśvatara Upanishads, thus reflecting back on a rather Christian conception of *brahman.* Only, the *modus operandi* is different from Christian grace.

Revelation, Harris thinks, if occurring at all in Hindu theology, is equivalent to the destruction of the individual,[84] and mediatorship there is none.[85] To us, however,

---

81 *Cf. The Chautauquan,* Vol. VI, p. 193; *National Education Association Proceedings,* 1889, p. 653; *New England Jour. of Ed.,* Vol. LVII, p. 5.

82 *Cf. Education,* Vol. XI, p. 267.

83 *Cf. Fifty-fifth Annual Meeting, etc.,* pp. 40 f.

84 *Cf. Education,* Vol. XI, p. 267; *Jour. Spec. Phil.,* Vol. XV, p. 208.

85 *Cf. Education,* Vol. XI, p. 269.

the much-discussed eleventh chapter of the Bhagavad Gītā seems to be a distinct case of revelation and mediatorship for Kṛṣṇa, the divine-human companion, servant and teacher of Arjuna, reveals to his pupil his noumenal form. In this case, at least, the divine gave substance and subsistence to the finite.

The space-time problem in Indian pantheism, Harris would say,[86] is non-existent, because these two forms belong to *māyā*. "The highest religion makes time and space a veritable cradle for the culture and education of individuals." [87] The vicissitudes of these concepts, even in Western thought, are well known; and if we regard *māyā* as the phenomenal we can assert, without knowing the literature, that the Hindus have occupied themselves thoroughly with the problem of space and time. The concept of causality, likewise, forms a large part of the discussions in Brahmanical as well as Buddhistic literature, and is not as subordinate as it would seem to be.[88]

The Hindus were never wont to carry ethical distinctions and changing moral ideas over into their absolute. Harris is, therefore, justified when he says that the ideas of righteousness and goodness can as little be permitted to apply to *brahman,* as those of wickedness and evil.[89] As Emerson had so magnificently shown in his poem "Brahma" (Harris censors him for that), the Hindu metaphysical principle is beyond good and evil. But we are not so sure that the ethical problem was discarded simply as a result of the *māyā*-doctrine.[90]

---

[86] Cf. *The Arena,* Vol. XVII, p. 355; *Educational Review,* Vol. XXIX, p. 28.

[87] *The Arena,* Vol. XVII, p. 355.

[88] Cf., e.g., *Educational Review,* Vol. XXIX, p. 29.

[89] Cf. *The Chautauquan,* Vol. III, p. 262; *Poet-Lore,* Vol. 1, p. 257; *Educational Review,* Vol. XXIX, pp. 24 f.

[90] Cf. *Psychologic Foundations,* pp. 276 f.

The firmest believers in *māyā,* the followers of Buddha, are also the most persistent in their demands upon a personal morality.   Harris himself acknowledges the moral precocity of the Hindu wise men who established codes and rules for conduct, such as the Hitopadeśa.   He there followed Emerson without sharing his enthusiasm.   "The ethical views of Asia were developed early, because the need was great for personal good behavior from those in authority." [91]   "The moral precocity of its wise men must not blind us to the compensating defect which is its occasion." [92]

The remarkable thing in Harris is that, with his puritanical sense of religious righteousness, he appreciated the ethical leaders of the East without criticism.   He accepted their moral ideals at their face value.   He used Emerson's "algebraic formulas," [93] but he draws a line between the wise men of the East and those of Greece, as they come from a different background.   "Confucius, Mencius, Zoroaster, Saadi, Vyasa, Gautama, Patanjali, and their peers are ethically inspired, so to speak.   The self-returning nature of human activity reveals itself in their minds with all the vividness of original insight.   But this flower-blossom of spiritual wisdom blooms in a moral desert wherein the people are sunk in abject slavery and do not realize as yet a sense of responsibility as individuals." [94]—Is not all country flat if seen from a mountain-top, we might ask?

The worth and dignity of the individual, Harris thought, is an idea attained only by Christianity.   The nihilistic Orient, the Orient that craves for absorption in

---

[91] *Atlantic Monthly,* Vol. L, p. 250.

[92] *Outline. Cf. The Western,* Vol. III, pp. 210 f.

[93] The enumeration of outstanding names or "magnitudes" in the spiritual world.

[94] *The Western,* Vol. I, p. 638.

an overpowering, impersonal might, can have no regard for individuality, can have no feeling, no love for one's neighbor. The transcendental deduction of Oriental despotism was thus accomplished. Henceforth, India is seen only *sub specie tyrannidis.* The saintly images of an Aśoka or Akbar do not rise at all above the Indian plain, at most the "lofty idea of female character" in Sitā,[95] the Indian Helen,[96] or Damayantī.[95]

Despotism is rampant. ". . . The will and the intellect are not yet, in the Orient, so far developed as to present the modern contrast of theoretical and practical. . . . The arbitrary will of the despot (whether in state, church, the family or the community) everywhere prevails; there is no constitutional limitation of the will of the tyrant of the State, or code of laws to limit the will of the other species of Tyrants. The only amelioration of this condition lies in the personal sense of justice, or the magnanimity of the ruler or master. Hence the wise men of China, India and Persia have left ethical treatises rather than philosophemes seeking to curb the arbitrary will by moral principles and to kindle the sense of duty in the minds of the rulers and masters. . . . The lack of established institutions of justice in the shape of civil laws and constitutions produces the intensity of moral inspiration which we see in such teachers as Confucius, Mencius, Zoroaster, Saadi, Vyasa, Gautama, Patanjali, and their peers." [97] Elsewhere Harris mentions the code of Manu and especially the Hitopadeśa. Such books as the Kautilya Arthaśāstra were, of course, not known to him.

---

95 *Cf. The Western,* Vol. III, p. 335.
96 *Cf. The Western,* Vol. I, p. 640.
97 *Outline. Cf.* also *The Theory of Education. School Room Classics,* Vol. XV (Syracuse, 1893), p. 23 (first published in 1870); *Atlantic Monthly,* Vol. L, p. 239; *U.S. Bureau of Education, Circulars of Information,* No. 3, p. 34; *Jour. of Soc. Sci.,* No. 20, Pt. II, p. 8; *Hegel's Logic,* p. 105.

"Given the religious ideal of the Chinese or Hindoo, and only despotic states can come from it." [98]   And again, the process works backwardly. "Where despotism prevails it is important that the ruler be a moral man, and that the subject be able to take refuge within the depths of his moral consciousness against the inevitable personal wrong done to his manhood. He must be able to renounce all happiness and like a Stoic find happiness in complete renunciation." [99]

On the one hand, Harris vigorously defends the Christian mainstay that morality exists only in virtue of the conception of a moral deity,[100] while, on the other hand, he rather inconsistently lodges a complaint against the fact that much of Oriental philosophy busies itself with morality. [101]   But, then, we must remember that he is a disciple of Hegel principally because Hegel justifies Christian thinking.[102]

Seen thus through the veil of history and the haze of distance, Harris deems the political situation in the Orient "at once a glory and a disgrace." [103]   He congratulates ourselves on having outgrown this phase in which "all government is conducted by irresponsible rulers" and "the happiness of the people depends entirely on the wisdom and moderation of the despot." "It is comparatively of little moment with us whether the sovereign is amiable or not." [104]   So great was his faith in our age that he not only denied the compatibility of striving for improvement

---

98 *Education,* Vol. I, p. 373.

99 *The Western,* Vol. III, pp. 210 f. *Cf.* Harris' discussion of *Die Formen der Ethik* in *Jour. of Spec. Phil.,* Vol. XV, p. 202.

100 *Cf. Educational Review,* Vol. X, p. 77 and elsewhere.

101 Already in *Outline;* see above.

102 *Cf. Jour. of Spec Phil.,* Vol. XV, p. 252.

103 *The Western,* Vol. I, p. 638.

104 *Atlantic Monthly,* Vol. L, p. 350.

with the conception of the divine in Eastern thinking,[105] but went further than Hegel who places the beginning of progress in the Orient, when he declared that progress is "from Asiatic tyranny to European and American democracy." [106]

By his numerous activities Harris was prevented from making a closer study of India's history and social and economic conditions. We, therefore, look in vain for enlivening references to Hindu life. It is all abstract and general. Even the Hindu weavers who weave "fine muslin at the rate of a single web of cloth in a lifetime" [107] are faintly drawn. Alexander's march to India epitomized to him a great spiritual conquest which we now realize was not and may never be completed.

However, he becomes somewhat more eloquent in speaking of the Yogin [108] who does not seek to beautify his body and thus to realize the divine-human in himself, but, through mortification of the flesh, shriveling up the body, paralyzing his muscles and producing numbness simulates his unconscious, "inhuman" ultimate. That these exhibitions of holiness are not Yoga in any of its branches, but the doings of madmen, is apparent to anyone who has studied Patañjali's Yogasūtras, or even the Gherandasaṁhitā or other Haṭhayoga treatises. In the former, Yoga is a mental discipline, in the latter a physical training, while in none is the aim other than consciousness supreme. There are fine passages in Harris' writings dealing with *bhakti*, *jñāna* and *karma* Yoga in the Bhagavad Gītā to be men-

---

105 *Cf.* Kies' *Selections*, p. 240.
106 *Psychologic Foundations*, p. 281.
107 *Education*, Vol. I, pp. 624 f.
108 *Cf. The Chautauquan*, Vol. VI, p. 193; *National Education Assn. Proc.* 1889, p. 653; *The Philosophic Aspects of History; Education*, Vol. XI, p. 267; *Psychologic Foundations*, pp. 276-7, 279, 360; *New England Jour. of Ed.*, Vol. LVII, p. 5; *Educational Review*, Vol. XXIX, p. 25.

tioned below.   The meaning and relation between these
forms of Yoga apparently were not very clear to our author's mind.

In his interpretation of art Harris follows Hegel's
Aesthetik throughout with its typical three-fold division
into symbolic, classical, and Romantic or Christian art.
Hindu art is symbolic and shows, in Harris' view, the char-
acteristics which are to be expected if the negative Absolute
finds expression in matter.[109]   We can, therefore, be brief
with Harris' estimate of Indian art and put it in the form
of a summary.

A crushing might in the shape of matter finds the
individual "embarrassed"; man seems to be nothing and
nature everything, and now an "ineffectual" struggle
against environment, against nature ensues.   It is a "vain,
impotent struggle" against this rude, unconscious force,
and the individual is unable to achieve freedom.   There is
only incessant repetition of trivial particulars, there are
no forms of free movement.   Freedom and individuality do
not find expression, they are crushed out.   The divine-
human cannot be portrayed, beauty is not attained, the symbols are not analogous to life, being mountains, rivers,
natural forces, destructive of individuality.   Either the
unity arrived at is too abstract, forbidding ornament, or
variety is too bewildering, being unable to reflect unity.
Architecture is clumsy, sculpture presents faces without
"conscious dignity and the repose of the soul."   Thus, the
works of art in the Orient "adumbrate or hint at what

---

109 For Harris' discussions of Hindu art *cf. The Chautauquan,* Vol. II,
pp. 135-329, and Vol. VI, pp. 192 f.; *National Ed. Assn. Proc.,* 1889,
pp. 651-654; 1897, pp. 263, 334-5; *U. S. Bureau of Education. Arts and Industry.* Part II (1892), pp. 1313-1315; *A. Bronson Alcott,* Vol. II, p. 597; *Report
of the Commissioner of Education,* 1898-9, Vol. I, pp. 688, 693-5; *Psychologic
Foundations,* pp. 273, 360, 368; *Kies' Selections,* pp. 196-7, 207, 235; Preface
to Vol. XXVIII of *International Education Series,* p. viii.

they do not adequately express." Once only a keen observation is made by Harris. Hindu art, he says, is "essentially the portrayal of incessant incarnation of vitality." [110]

Harris, today, could not for a moment maintain his thesis. That Hindu art is symbolic is admitted by all connoisseurs. But that it lacks gracefulness, abounds in stiff lines, shows lack of harmony, or even does not possess an appreciation for the beauties of nature and of the body needs no specific refutation. We simply point to Ajaṇta, Sāñchī, Anurādhapura, Buddhagayā, Gāndhāra as centers of ancient Buddhistic art. We do not wish to begin enumerating the strangely fascinating indigenous art, the priceless works of art in the Mohammedan period, or the exquisite productions of the modern Renaissance, especially in painting.

The intrinsic virtues of Oriental art require deeper standards than loveliness and gracefulness. And if freedom from the body—as Hegel's highest category of art—be applied as a criterion, we might discover it rather in Oriental than in Christian, Romantic art, but above all in the figure of the Buddha. We may, therefore, pass over Harris' esthetic criticism. The void absolute seems to us to be ill reflected in the colorful and over-rich art treasures of India still little known in Harris' days. It would rather strike us that whatever art-products we possess and unearth show us an abundance of conscious soul, even where *māyā* is pictured in the fulness of nature, as in the friezes and frescoes illustrating the stories of the Rāmāyaṇa and the Jātakas.

In the social life of India Harris again finds his funda-

---

[110] Kies, *Selections*, p. 235.

mental assumption of a negative unity underlying Hindu
thought illustrated in the caste-system. This gives him
also occasion to treat of Hindu education, because caste
and education are reciprocal.[111] His criticism of caste is
confined mainly to the statement that it is an accompany-
ing phenomenon of despotic states and places limits upon
the infinite possibilities of the individual by allowing birth
(an accident of nature) to determine one's life, which is
thus over-shadowed by a web of fate. It entails a most
complex system of duties, such as tedious ceremonies of
purification which prevent mobility as an essential factor
in human development and constitute such a burden that
life is no longer considered worth living. So weighed
down by formalities is the poor Hindu that he "looked at
one of his temples cut of solid rock, and saw the symbol of
himself standing there as one of the human columns sup-
porting the roof and the mountain over it." [112]

This criticism is, of course, not only poetic, but psychologically untenable. A criticism of caste must involve the
whole of the Hindu outlook in order to be accurate.[113]
However, we are not a little astonished at the dispassionate
remarks of Harris regarding an institution so totally foreign to the American point of view. He saw deeper than
most who at his time condemned out and out the Hindus
for their caste.

---

111 Cf. the discussions in the following: Jour. of Spec. Phil., Vol. III,
pp. 181 f. and Vol. IV, p. 102; National Ed. Assn. Proc., 1874, p. 80
(same passages reprinted elsewhere as late as 1890) ; 1885, p. 493; The Western, Vol. II, (1874), p. 128, and Vol. III (n.s. 1877), pp. 212-213, 236; The
Chautauquan, Vol. III, pp. 194-196; New England Jour. of Ed., Vol. XVI,
pp. 227-228, 265; Special Report of the Bureau of Education. Nat. Exhibits
and Conventions at the World's Industrial and Cotton Centennial Exposition,
New Orleans, 1884-5. Part II, pp. 478 f.; Forum, Vol. IV, p. 578; Educational
Review, Vol. VII, p. 9; Psychologic Foundations, pp. 275-6, 277; International
Education Series, Vol. I, p. viii, and Vol. II, pp. viii f.; et al. loc.

112 Kies, Selections, p. 196.

113 Cf. my article, Int. Jour. of Ethics, Vol. XLIII, pp. 183-193.

Harris correctly thought that every employment becomes an occasion for caste and the distinction of moral codes. In so doing, India apotheosized, as it were, civil society and its division of labor. For, division of labor is necessary for gaining skill in conquering nature. It is, therefore, understandable that the Hindus regard division of labor "the great divine fact of life."

The distinction which Harris draws between class and caste is exceedingly shallow so that the phenomenon of "clashes" in Europe generally and in England in particular, caused him not inconsiderable trouble.[114] As an American, he feared that even special education for physicians and lawyers might lead to a Brahman caste [115] and that science with its pantheistic tendencies would have its legitimate outcome in an Indian caste-system.[116] But as a friend of Great Britain he subdued his view that the English are mistaken in fostering caste-feeling, and acknowledged the necessary and admirable features of caste for the British Islander. Thus, the British East India Company is one device "invented by the unconscious spirit of the people to make the higher ranks, the hereditary nobility, and the possessions of wealth founded on monopolies, serve the lower ranks of the people." It spares no expenditure of wealth and military power, and "all for the creation of opportunity for the average common citizen." [117]

It is the school that perpetuates the social institutions. Hence, education in India is designed to maintain caste. Harris says that the Hindu would not educate beyond the

---

114 Cf. *New England Jour. of Ed.,* Vol. V, pp. 18 f. and Vol. XVI, p. 228; *U. S Bureau of Education. Art and Industry.* Pt. II (1892), p. 594 (first published, 1882) ; *Educational Review,* Vol. XVII, p. 316; *International Education Series,* Vol. XXII, p. vi, and Vol. LVI, pp. x ff.

115 Cf. *Fifty-fourth Annual Meeting, etc.,* p. 143.

116 Cf. *North-American Review,* Vol. CXXXI, p. 245.

117 *International Education Series,* Vol. LVI, p. xv.

position of birth and that his system of education would extend only over knowledge, duties and virtues compatible with the particular caste. Roughly speaking, this is true, though it has not always been the case in history. We know of exceptions. Likewise, low-caste men and women have not always been excluded from education. In fact, we find passages in literature reporting communication of the highest *brahma*-knowledge to worthy Sūdras, as well as philosophical debates with women of rare attainments, and we are under no compulsion to assume that they were bayaderes.

The process of Brahmanical instruction is interestingly described by Harris. The teacher is honored. He is a Brahman "devoted to spiritual direction," he is "the illumination, the revelation and exposition." A god to others he teaches the Vedas, morality in the shape of fables from the Hitopadeśa, philosophy, duties, ceremonials, reading, writing and arithmetic to the twice-born boy. As a mark of respect the pupil puts the foot of the teacher on his head, is careful to pronounce the holy syllable *"om"* to insure right success and learns his lessons by the "monitorial" system. Letters are first written in sand, then with an iron pencil on palm-leaves. One child assists the other in learning, and they all reside with the teacher in a sort of boarding school.

The ultimate aim of Hindu education is, of course, not extinction in any negative unity, neither the "abnegation of all that looks toward the recognition of identity of human nature and the equality of all in the substance of manhood." This is a natural, but fallacious interpretation of caste. We should likewise be cautious in asserting that truth-saying is not much thought of and that evil is taught to be looked upon as *māyā*.[118] Somewhat "abstract" contemplation and meditation are, indeed, encouraged, and a Brahman is free from any menial tasks to lead a life of study and repose. The relativity of standards is also generally recognized, so that what is virtue in one caste is a sin in another, although this too must be taken *cum grano salis.*

Under the influence of his own views concerning the divine-human Harris complains that the Hindus would spare animal life even in tigers, serpents, scorpions and vermin and maintain hospitals for monkeys and cows, but are indifferent to the sufferings of humanity.[119] The ideal of *ahiṃsā*, non-injury to any living creature, was, no doubt, transferred also to humans. Has not Ayurveda, the science of medicine, been cultivated extensively in India at all times, even though of course not with the efficiency of twentieth-century knowledge?

It is most significant for our study of Harris that apparently his occupation with the educational ideas of the Orient as well as his knowledge of literature had a determining influence on his own pedagogical views, at least in one significant point. As he himself acknowledges in an interesting passage: [120] "On learning to see this question of language-study in the light of the evolution of civilization, I came to understand why the Chinese lay so much stress on the study of the writings of Confucius and Mencius, and why the high-caste youths of India study Sanskrit. I have long since abandoned my objections to the tra-

---

118 *Cf. John Hopkins University Studies in Historical and Political Science*, Vol. XI, (1893), p. 269 and *Psychologic Foundations*, p. 276.

119 *Cf. The Chautauquan*, Vol. III, p. 195, and Vol. VI, p. 193; *New England Jour. of Ed.*, Vol. XVI, p. 265; *National Education Association Proceedings*, 1889, p. 654; *Psychologic Foundations*, p. 277.

120 *Educational Review*, Vol. VII, p. 9.

ditional education of Latin and Greek in colleges and academies."

The importance of this passage is realized by anyone who knows that the adolescent Harris, disgusted with his classical training, repudiated strongly this phase of modern education, while the teacher, superintendent and Commissioner Harris vigorously broke a lance for instruction in Latin and Greek. His position he defended skilfully. Both languages are required to understand our own cultural background. The Hindu also studies his Sanskrit literature, because it is necessary for his self-knowledge. He learns the Hitopadeśa, the Vedas and the Purāṇas in order "to become conscious of the ideal principles of his caste-system." In this connection it is not unadvised to call attention to the fact that Harris recognized the importance of the Indian village community for Hindu cultural life, although in another place he hails the city as the true focus of civilization.

The phenomenon of Buddhism was explained by Harris in its origin as a "reaction against the religion of caste, which posits rigid distinctions between classes of men." It put dynamite under and subverted the tyranny of caste,[121] replacing the "aristocracy of the caste-system by a monastic democracy." [122] Under Buddhism all families have a chance "to ascend to the highest state of religious culture." [123] The burdensome brahmanical ceremonies are done away with; all the rest of the inacceptable implications of Brahmanism are left intact. So, Buddhism is destructive of individualism, is pantheistic in outlook,

---

[121] Cf. Outline; Jour. of Spec. Phil., Vol. XI, p. 443-4; The Western, Vol. I, p. 635, and Vol. III, pp. 212 f; New England Jour. of Ed., Vol. XVI, p. 228; Psychologic Foundations, p. 276.

[122] Outline.

[123] The Chautauquan, Vol. III, p. 196.

makes science impossible and does not reach the concept of personality. Although an ancient nihilism,[124] it is close to modern materialism.[125]

Harris is sometimes unmindful of the ideals of *ahiṁsā* so pronounced in Buddhism, as when he writes that Buddhist life "strives to attain the extinction of self-interest as well as interest in others." [126] Nevertheless, he has to acknowledge that it "presents lovely phases to our view continually. But its fatal defect is its utter incapacity to develop out of itself and in harmony with itself a three-fold secular life—family, society, and the State."[127]

The central idea of Buddhism, *nirvāṇa*, Harris variously interpreted as a subjective state, quietistic repose, the drowning of sorrow, absolute indifference, ceasing of change and practical absorption. As such he recognized an identity with the *mokṣa* of the Sāṅkya. It is also the "rest of unconsciousness" and implies a doubtful recognition of immortality.

Our author early became familiar with the two views of *nirvāṇa,* either as "annihilation of the soul" or "conquest over our animal passions and desires, the annihilation of the animal for the benefit of the spirit." [128] Doubtless, it was mainly Max Müller's *Lecture on Buddhist Nihilism,* which he reviewed in the *Journal of Speculative Philosophy,*[129] that acquainted him with these differences in opinion. It is to be regretted deeply that Harris turned away altogether from a positive interpretation of *nirvāṇa* as

---

124 Cf. *New England Jour. of Ed.,* Vol. XVI, p. 228.

125 Cf. *Jour. of Spec. Phil.,* Vol. X, p. 330.

126 *Psychologic Foundations,* p. 276.

127 *Jour. of Spec. Phil.,* Vol. XI, pp. 442 ff., in a review of Mills' *The Indian Saint; or, Buddha and Buddhism.*

128 *The Western,* Vol. I, p. 647.

129 Vol. IX, pp. 104 f.

the *summum bonum.* He even cites the Sanskrit *śānti,* peace, bliss, happiness, which is often the equivalent of *nirvāṇa,* but he does not adopt it in his interpretation.

The admirable feature of Harris always remains the matter-of-factness in his exposition even if his own views are radically different. This certainly constitutes an alleviating circumstance in his habitual neglect of inconvenient facts. He himself may have been caught during his "antemundane soul-wandering" [130] in the meshes of "Esoteric Buddhism" and "theosophy" which he so often mentions in his writings. Their dangers to Christianity were later perfectly plain to him when he came to realize the potential influence of parallels that may be drawn between the doctrine as well as the life of a Buddha and the teachings and the walk of Christ. *The Light of Asia* was especially persuasive and even today has not lost its power. Harris, therefore, recognized it as his duty to show that Buddhism is *toto coelo* different from Christianity.

Summing up his criticism,[131] the following salient points appear: Christianity, over against Buddhism, is positive, allows the secular to develop itself, and is less ascetic, while Buddhism has less frightful penances than Brahmanism. Comparative religion seems to fail, according to Harris, when it maintains that Christianity and Buddhism hold the same truths. The fact is that Buddhism is "infinitely below" Christianity, because it is supposed to slight the divine in man and reject will, feeling, love and consciousness for its highest reality, which lacks the character of personality, form, self-revelation, self-

---

130 *The College and the Church* (New York, 1887), p. 59.

131 *Cf. Jour. of Spec. Phil.,* Vol. II, p. v; Vols. XI, pp. 434 f.; XXI, pp. 359 f., 417. Also *The Chautauquan,* Vol. III, p. 196; *Jour. Soc. Sci.,* No. 15, pp. 1 f.; *International Education Series,* Vol. I, p. viii; *Hegel's Logic,* p. 301; *Education,* Vol. XI, pp. 266 ff.; *Educational Review,* Vol. XXIX, pp. 24, 29.

distinction and goodness. This last quality of the divine in Christianity is "so gracious as to create and give independent reality to nature and man—in short, to make man able to sin and to defy the First Cause, his Creator." Consequently, a Buddhist may be converted to Christianity only when he has changed completely his "intellectual mode of viewing things." This holds good, of course, even to a larger extent with respect to Brahmanism.

Interesting is the fact that Harris associates in his mind Buddhism with the Sāṅkhya, because there are certain similarities, especially in the matter of caste.[132] Also the lapse from "primeval unity which is not subject and object" into consciousness (see our discussion and correction above) he regards "the basis of the religion of Buddhism." [133] Likewise, *mokṣa* and the whole theory connected with it is not recognized by Harris as universally Hindu, for he thinks it peculiar to the Sāṅkhya, the Yoga, and Buddhism.[134]

Harris did not dwell on the dualistic approach of the Sāṅkhya with its two principles of *puruṣa* and *prakṛti*. In *Johnson's Cyclopaedia,* the Sāṅkhyan scholar, Richard Garbe, discussed this philosophy, but Harris, also a contributor, did not revise his earlier views. At one time he reprinted the aphorisms of Kapila, in Colebrooke's translation, in the *Journal of Speculative Philosophy* [135] and quoted liberally from them afterwards.

In his first enthusiasm he yet called Kapila the profoundest of East Indian thinkers,[136] for he seemed to set

---

132 *Cf. Jour. of Spec. Phil.,* Vol. XI, pp. 443 f.; *Psychologic Foundations,* p. 276.

133 *Educational Review,* Vol. XXIX, pp. 28 f.

134 *Cf. Outline.*

135 Vol. II, pp. 225-229; *cf. ibid.,* p. iv, as well as *Outline* and *The Western,* Vol I, pp. 642 ff.

136 In *Jour. of Spec. Phil.,* Vol. XI, p. 265.

a fundamental problem and solve it with insight. Relief from pain, the vicissitudes of bodily life and the decrees of fate, are discovered in knowledge, "in the timeless and spaceless thinking which gazes upon the true in-and-for-itself."[137] This formulation reminds us of German idealism, and Harris adds later on: ". . . We see the solution of the Hindu sage, Kapila, was not out of the way. So far as man is a twofold being, spirit and matter, he feels and perceives the limitation and constraint which his body involves. Hence he is a being of suffering and pain inherently. But this solution lies in ascending into the universal activity of Mind on the one hand, and on the other in recognizing his Species so as to form a new externality for himself that shall shut out the rude shocks of merely natural force and body, from himself. Kapila did not see the latter side or the realization of freedom, but he did see the former or the actualization of freedom through pure thought or insight into truth." [138]

Harris had thus discovered in true knowledge or understanding—*vidyā* and *jñāna,* in Sanskrit—the essence of one of the major systems of Indian philosophy. Insight "annihilates" "all particular things and beings through reflection" [139] and insures "freedom from the root of egotism." [140]

Having gone that far, Harris was well on the road to a complete understanding of Indian philosophy. He himself saw the cross-roads, for plainly he states the case in his outline of Oriental philosophy. He poses the question as to whether the Sānkhyan solution of the knowledge

---

137 *Ibid.*

138 *Ibid.,* p. 270. *Cf.* further already Vol. II, p. iv and *The Western,* Vol. I, pp. 642, 649.

139 *The Chautauquan,* Vol. III, p. 196.

140 *A. Bronson Alcott,* Vol. II, pp. 658 f.

problem means "annihilation and absorption of the soul into the nothingness of the absolute" or gives expression to the theory "that when mind recognizes the external world to be phenomenal" the soul is cognizant of the fundamental truth, ceases to wander about in error and dispells *māyā*.

The significance of this passage cannot be over-estimated. Had he adopted the last view, Harris would have held the master key in his hands that would have unlocked all Indian thought and showered its treasures into his lap. At the same time he would have had to fling aside the exclusiveness of theological speculation and his theory of the dialectic of Christianity and Orientalism.

There is the problem of *māyā,* for instance. When Harris speaks of *māyā* in the sense of delusion of untutored reflection or illusion of the senses merely, of the dualism (*māyā*) of ex-istence which must be com-prehended or grasped together, and when he speaks of the *māyā* of thought, including the abstract categories, concepts and laws which must pass through the fire of the dialectic [141]— then we have in such Hegelian phraseology a correct use of *māyā*.

Yoga, too, may be met with on a higher plane than that of mimicing the ungraceful and numb absolute in some absurd posture. Though Harris' mentioning of this higher type of Yoga is brief, it is tolerably correct. He characterizes Patañjali's system as avoidance of temptation, renunciation, quietism and contemplative asceticism.[142] The *Karmayoga* of the Bhagavad Gītā, he tells us, "enjoins the

---

141 *Cf. Jour. of Spec. Phil.,* Vol. III, pp. 287 f.; Vol. IV, p. 95; Vol. XI, p. 436.

142 *Cf. The Western,* Vol. I, p. 641; *Outline; The Genius and Character of Emerson,* p. 378; *Educational Review,* Vol. XXIX, p. 27.

combatting of temptation and arms its devotees for the active contest with evil." [143]

About this latter type of Yoga Harris even waxes eloquent. He derives it—as practically everything he deems worthwhile—from the Sāṅkhya.[144] In the Bhagavad Gītā he sees it as fifteen different kinds of devotion, "the highest of which is the devotion as regards emancipation and renunciation through true knowledge. Works become indifferent in this stage as far as self-interest is concerned, but are performed solely in the interest of the Eternal Purpose." [145] Now he brings a passage from Goethe's *Wilhelm Meister's Travels* in support of the emancipation of knowledge and culture.

Furthermore, the *karman* doctrine is here implicated and treated appreciatively in the following words: "It is most noteworthy that the Karma Yoga holds that all actions are mystically connected with their results, so that from the moment the act is concluded, the agent acquires a mystic virtue which he does not lose until in this or the next existence the reward of the action is administered to him. This approaches the Christian doctrine of responsibility. As Dante portrays it (and Hawthorne too in his novels) a man's deed is accompanied by a spiritual atmosphere. Man enters this atmosphere at once with the commission of the deed. This is the first return upon him of his act, which if wicked creates for him his *Inferno*. Then if he struggles to emancipate himself from his deeds by aspiration to the holy, the process is *Purgatorio*. Or indeed the mediating effect of the pain of the Inferno, is

---

143 *The Western,* Vol. I, p. 641; *cf. Outline.*

144 *Cf. The Western,* Vol. I, pp. 649 ff.

145 *Ibid. Cf.* also the review of the Bhagavad Gītā in *Jour. of Spec. Phil.,* Vol. IX, p. 336.

purgatorial. The just deed brings with it the atmosphere of the *Paradiso*." [146]

This is one of the very few allusions in Harris to the fundamental and universal *karman* doctrine. The parallel with Dante is extremely suggestive. In another place *karman* is brought in connection with the kind of immortality of species which the pantheistic scientist associates with hereditary transmission and personal influence beyond the grave.[147] It may be useful to call attention to Harris' doctrine of grace and justice (as the principle of grace applied to free beings)[148] and to compare it with *karman,* or, the return of the deed upon the doer according to his capacity.

The usual criticism of Hindu thought concentrates upon *karman* as a heartless doctrine and *sainsara* as an absurdity. The more we are surprised that Harris makes hardly mention of either as typically Hindu concepts. Even *samsāra,* again understood as originally a *Sāṅkhyan* concept, coincides for him merely with the mundane life and ceases with *māyā* dispelled.

In conjunction with the Viṣṇu Purāṇa, from which he cited freely, Harris developed a positive interpretation of the Sāṅkhya which leaves behind his customary view of annihilation and absorption of all individuality in an empty absolute.[149]

Five approaches, rather than stages, are noted in the process that "lets matter perish and soul live." One is that all externality, nature, must be excluded from the realm of truth in order that the soul may attain spirituality. We

---

146 *Ibid.,* p. 650.
147 *Cf. Jour. of Spec. Phil.,* Vol. XIX, pp. 192 f.
148 *Cf. ibid.,* Vol. VIII, p. 187, and Vol. XV, pp. 210 f.
149 *Cf. The Western,* Vol I, pp. 644-646.

are thinking of *māyā* and *prakṛti* here when Harris shrewdly says: "The negation of nature is the negation of negation and hence true affirmation. Negation of the finite is the infinite."

Again, when the phenomenal character of nature is disclosed, the ultimate presupposition of *māyā* remains in the shape of a self-moving or self-determining subject. "Thus the soul pierces through nature to find the necessary logical condition thereof in a subject or ego. In short, soul finds itself under nature; reason finds reason, and thus comes through nature to itself—returns through the object to subject. This process is the eternal 'Phenomenology of Mind', as Hegel names it." We are told to compare Emerson's "Nature" in the *Miscellanies*.

Further, with the discovery of generic processes, specific existence and knowledge looking only for it ("discriminative knowledge") vanish, and "only the soul abides with its power of self-discrimination."

Starting with the view that man's mind is the cause of liberation as well as bondage, we ascend from reflection, as the lowest form of thought which discloses dependence and correlation merely, into speculative thinking. Here we comprehend and synthesize and find the ultimate to be "self-uttering or self-manifesting, repelling itself from itself, as it were. Hence it is subject or pure ego." Soul is thus liberated through mind.

Finally, from the transitory nature of the distinctions in the external world, the soul may also recognize "its own superior essence."

After such a keen exegesis of Hindu thought the statement aforementioned is made that although the outcome of Hindu philosophy is usually regarded as "pure all-absorbing nihilism," one may interpret it as expressing "a truly spiritual theory which attributes immortality to the soul and supreme personality to God."

For the interrelation of the major systems of Brahmanical philosophy and the unorthodox Buddhism, Harris apparently had to rely throughout on most inadequate sources. In the Bhagavad Gītā, to which we shall now turn, this is less obvious. However, here too we shall pass over some errors and inaccuracies. For, after all, in investigations of this kind the ideal values gathered from the Hindu sources constitute the centre of interest and influence.

It was in 1872 that Harris read the Bhagavad Gītā for the first time. In 1875 he wrote a review of Thompson's translation for the *Journal of Speculative Philosophy* and published a solid article entitled "Oriental Philosophy and the Bhagavad Gita" in *The Western*. Whenever he referred to Emerson's poem "Brahma" he pointed out its original in the Gītā, and in the lectures at the Concord School of Philosophy (later edited by F. B. Sanborn as *The Genius and Character of Emerson*) he made a detailed study of the parallels in the verses of both. In fact, he regarded the New England Brahman's poem "a wholly admirable epitome, or condensed statement, of that wonderful book," the Bhagavad Gītā. Its whole substance he saw pressed into four short verses, furnishing "a surprising contrast in its terseness to the tedious recapitulation in Oriental literature."

Whoever has studied the infiltration of Hindu lore and mind into American literature will agree with Harris that Wilkins' 1785 translation of the Bhagavad Gītā was the source "whence the current ideas regarding Indian philosophy have come." [150] He characterized it as a remark-

---

150 *Outline.*

able episode of the Mahābhārata, containing "nearly all of the grand mysteries of the Brahmanic religion," a "good compend of East Indian philosophy"; yes, he recommended it to all those desirous of knowing something of the flavor of East Indian idealism.

Doctrine and setting of the *Song of the Blessed One* were discussed by Harris; but since the spiritual content presents all the main features of Hindu thought they need not be reiterated here. Yet, the vision of the universal form justly claims some notice. It is fully treated by our author in an article entitled "Goethe's 'World Spirit' and the Vishnu of the 'Bhagavad Gita'." [151] Let us have Harris speak for himself.

"In the eleventh chapter of the 'Bhagavad Gita' there is portrayed the 'Vision of the Universal Form.' It is the sublimest portion of that work. Arjuna, in answer to his prayer, is suddenly endowed with the power to see the whole universe as a cosmic process of birth and decay. It is the body of Vishnu."

"The individual versus the universal is the subject alike of this passage of the Indian poem and of the first scene in 'Faust' as well." "In Goethe's 'Faust' there is a parallel passage in which the 'Erd-Geist' flashes before the blinded vision of the solitary student poring over the book of Nature."

"The form of the Universal is, indeed, very difficult to behold. It has to be represented as destructive of the individual. This eleventh chapter of the 'Bhagavad Gita' and the scene of the 'Erd-Geist' in Goethe's 'Faust' furnish us two similar poetic images designed to accomplish this exhibition of great negative world-processes which generate

---

151 In *Poet-Lore*, Vol. I, pp. 401-406; *cf.* also *Jour. of Spec. Phil.*, Vol. XI, p. 435.

individuals and again absorb them,—just as the ocean breaks into individual waves and then swallows them up again." There is also a parallel in Carlyle's chapter on "Natural Supernaturalism," in the *Sartor Resartus*.

Harris, however, sees the same Oriental shortcomings. While Goethe introduces this negative world-spirit as a contrast to the *Ewig-Weibliche* which symbolizes, according to him, the divine tenderness of God which Faust experiences after rejecting finally the tutelage of Mephistopheles, the Bhagavad Gītā "holds to the absorption of the individual in the absolute as the true goal."

The question may, perhaps, be raised as to whether this great, final experience, requiring perfect devotion, *bhakti*, is not, in its mystic goal and mystic operation, essentially identical in Orient and Occident.

Finally, in one further respect is the Bhagavad Gītā most important for Harris' attitude toward the Orient. It became the open sesame to all Indian Philosophy.

In 1873, one year after he had begun his study of the Bhagavad Gītā, he threw aside his Cousin and the other histories of philosophy and blamed them for having misguided him into the belief that there are different systems of thought at all to be found in India.[152] No Sanskrit scholars of the rank of Colebrooke, Wilkins or Weber, no authority of the native Hindu scholars could then convince him that "real differences of theory" existed between the Indian systems.[153] Even if he had known all six orthodox systems of philosophy and all the Buddhist, Jain and *Cārvāka* schools and even if he had distinguished between Vedas and Vedānta, it remains doubtful whether he would

---

152 *Cf. Books That Have Helped Me*, p. 23, and *Hegel's Logic*, p. xiii.
153 *Cf. Poet-Lore*, Vol. I, p. 254.

have altered his view that for fifteen years he had been deceived as to the real significance of Indian thought.

Here is his autobiographical statement. He is speaking about the years before 1860: "I had begun to adopt the view that differences belong to phenomena alone, while identity belongs to noumenon,—in other words, differences are superficial, identity is fundamental,—the many seem, the One is. I do not speak of this view as an ultimate one, or as the view I hold at present; it was the view that had begun to commend itself to me at that time as the principle with which to explain the world. I did not at that time know that this is the all-pervading doctrine of the Hindoo systems of thought." [154]

His thought had not ripened yet when he read Emerson's "Brahma," for he jotted down over the title of this poem "Pure Being," suggesting that he subscribed to exactly what the Hindus generally are interpreted as believing, without himself being conscious of it.[155]

The fatal insight that made him see all Hindu thought as one homogeneous mass and turn his back on it came after the reading of the Bhagavad Gītā. For the first time he saw, so he relates, "that the differences of systems were superficial, and that the First Principle pre-supposed and even explicitly stated by the Sanskrit writers was everywhere the same, and that this is the principle of Pure Being as the negative unity of all things." [156]

And he continues: "In this I came to see Hegel's deep discernment which early in this century, in the dawn of oriental study, had enabled him to penetrate the true essence of Hindoo thought even in the western wrappages

---

154 *Ibid.*
155 *Cf. ibid.,* p. 253.
156 *Hegel's Logic,* pp. xiii-xvi.

in which the European first discoverers had brought it away . . . Hegel's greatest aperçu is the difference between the oriental and occidental spirit of thinking and doing."

With Hegel as bolt the door was now securely barred between Orient and Occident. Henceforth, Harris could effectively promote the Christian cause, for the enemy was drawn up in a solid line from materialism and scientific pantheism to deism and Orientalism.

Far off, to the East, the Hindus continued to believe in one reality, approached in multifarious ways.

Harris, we believe, could not help but arrive at the typically Western view of the excluded middle. Contrasts and opposites moved the dialectic of his thought and moved the frontiers of civilizations. A conciliatory, synthetic view could not at that time be harmonized with a tremendously busy, forward-pushing, propagandizing American spirit. At Concord one could indulge in aloofness, but it was at Concord where Harris, comparatively speaking, failed. Given an enormous interest in things and people and inexhaustible energy, there was no constitutional alternative: the many and the personal *had to* become reality for him.

But success also implied riddance of any heathenish allegiance and positive adjustment to Christianity. The lesson of history is clear on that point. Harris, the philosopher and defender of the faith, rose triumphantly from school-teacher to the top of his profession. *In his person he embodied his thesis that Christianity is progress and civilization.*

Thus, India has lost out, yet contributed to the fame of Harris. She furnished him the invisible enemy that put him into his strategic position and justified the rigor of his

argument.   Had Harris not drawn the picture of the Indian world of thought so markedly, his own ideas would
have lacked their clarity, his own writings would have
lacked their driving force.   In Harris India suffered so
that America might become conscious of her mission.

BIBLIOGRAPHY: WILLIAM TORREY HARRIS IN LITERATURE

BIBLIOGRAPHY: WILLIAM TORREY HARRIS IN LITERATURE

BY KURT F. LEIDECKER

The following list of what has been written about Dr. Harris is selective. Nevertheless, with the kind aid of many persons it is believed to be representative. That so many have deemed it worth their while to discuss Dr. Harris' theories and accomplishments is ocular proof of the scope and magnitude of his contributions to American civilization. The list would, in fact, have swollen considerably if all the theses and dissertations in manuscript which have been offered in colleges and universities from New York and Washington, D. C. to Oregon and Texas had been included. But only he who has studied these writings will form an adequate conception of how singularly admired and beloved a man Dr. Harris was. Other suns are now above the horizon in the fields in which he labored. Yet, every careful student of the literature realizes how much light and warmth *he* spent.

The compiler wishes to thank heartily all persons who have so generously given of their time and information, in particular Miss Edith Davidson Harris, but for whose help a large number of important references might be missing, and Miss Edith A. Wright who, through the kind offices of Miss Sabra W. Vought, Chief of the Library Division of the U. S. Office of Education, also supplied a long list of valuable items. Additional references to writings about the life and work of Dr. Harris will be gratefully acknowledged.

Alcott, A. Bronson, *Sonnets and Canzonets* (Boston, 1882), Part II. The 12th sonnet is descriptive of W. T. Harris.

American College and Public School Directory, ed. C. H. Evans, V (St. Louis, 1883), 187-190: "William Torrey Haris, LL.D." Biography, with portrait.

American Education, XIII, 155 (Dec., 1909). Notice of Harris' death.

American Educational Review, XXXI, 179-180 (Dec., 1909). Obituary notice. *Cf.* p. 192.

American Monthly Review of Reviews, XXX, 325 (Sept., 1904). With portrait.

American School Commissioner, III, 399 (Dec., 1894), "Hon. W. T. Harris, U. S. Commissioner of Schools." With portrait.

Ames, Charles H., a tribute to W. T. Harris, *Jour. of Education,* LXX, 608 and 610 (Dec. 9, 1909).
— "William Torrey Harris," *Jour. of Phil., Psy. and Sci. Meth.,* VI, 701-9 (Dec. 23, 1909). *Cf.* the obituary notice on p. 672 (Nov. 25, 1909).

"Ariana", "The Concord School of Philosophy" in *Critic,* I, 199 (July 30, 1881).

Atlantic Educational Journal, V, 140 (Dec., 1909). Obituary notice.

Babcock, Madison, "Life and Educational Services of W. T. Harris," *California Educational Review,* I, 241-2 (June, 1891). With portrait.

Bailey, Henry Turner, reminiscences of W. T. Harris in *School Arts Book,* X, 989-993 (June, 1911).
— *Yankee Notions* (Cambridge, 1929), pp. 96-108: "Notion 9, That Contact with a Master Mind may have Transforming Power."

Bardeen, C. W., "William Torrey Harris," *School Bulletin,* XXXVI, 65-68 (Dec., 1909). With portrait. Includes letters to Bardeen in facsimile and the short notice of Harris' death in *Nation,* LXXXIX, 465 (Nov. 11, 1909).
— *A Dictionary of Educational Biography* (Syracuse, N. Y., 1901), p. 241. With portrait.

Barnard, Henry, "William Torrey Harris and St. Louis Public Schools," *American Journal of Education,* XXX (n.s. V), 625-640 (Sept., 1880).

Bates, Ernest Sutherland, "William Torrey Harris," *Dictionary of American Biography,* VIII (New York, 1932), 328-330.

Beale, Dorothea, and others, *Work and Play in Girls' Schools* (London, 1901). See Index s.v. Harris, Dr.

van Becelaere, L., *La Philosophie en Amérique depuis les Origines jusqu'à nos Jours (1607-1900)* (New York, 1904). This historical essay is dedicated to W. T. Harris *comme à l'un des plus zélés apôtres et pionniers des études philosophiques aux Etats-Unis,* and Harris' work is referred to throughout.

Blow, Susan E., "History of the Kindergarten," *Outlook,* LV, 932-938 (Apr. 3, 1897).
— "The Service of Dr. W. T. Harris to the Kindergarten," *International Kindergarten Union. Proceedings, 1910,* 123-143 (Woburn, Mass., 1910). Also in *Kindergarten Review,* XX, 589-603 (June, 1910).
— "In Memoriam: Dr. William Torrey Harris," *Kindergarten Review,* XX, 259-260 (Dec., 1909). *Cf.* p. 261.
— "Kindergarten Education," *Education in the United States,* ed. Nicholas Murray Butler (New York, Cincinnati, Chicago, 1910); on pp. 38-41 a discussion of Harris' Kindergarten Report.

Boone, Richard Gause, *Education in the United States* (New York, 1894). See Index under Harris, W. T.
— and Palmer, Frank H., editorial on the retirement of Dr. Harris as Commissioner of Education, *Education,* XXVII, 49-52 (Sept., 1906).

Boston Herald for Nov. 6, 1909. Obituary notice.

Bowen, Clarence Winthrop, *The History of Woodstock, Connecticut,* VI (Norwood, Mass., 1935) 701-4. With portrait. *Cf.* Vol. I (1926), Index.

Boykin, James C., editorial, "Trained Minds Bring Practical Benefit to Mankind," *School Life,* XII, 170 (May, 1927).

Brokmeyer, Henry C.,—see under Cary, Charles P.

Brosnahan, Timothy, *Dr. Harris, U. S. Commissioner of Education, and the Agnostic School House* (The Messenger, New York [1904]). 31 pp.

Brown, Elmer Ellsworth, "Address at the Funeral of Doctor Harris," *Educational Bi-monthly*, IV, 229-230 (Feb., 1910). Also in *Colorado School Journal*, XXV, 334-335 (Feb., 1910).
— "Tribute to Dr. Harris," *Kindergarten Primary Magazine*, XXII, 236-7 (Apr., 1910).
— "A Message from the United States Bureau of Education," *Jour. of Education*, LXXII, 8-9 (July 7, 1910).
— —see under Brown, George Pliny, *Providence*, (R. I.), *Daily Journal*, and Winship, Albert E.

Brown, George Pliny, "William Torrey Harris," *School and Home Education*, XXIX, 103-107 (Dec., 1909).
— "In Memoriam—William Torrey Harris," *National Education Association. Proceedings of the Department of Superintendence. Indianapolis, March 1-3, 1910*, pp. 47-52. Brown died Feb. 1, 1910, and the paper was read by John W. Cook, with introduction. It is the first paper of three, the others being by Charles P. Cary on pp. 52-57, who quoted Brokmeyer, and Elmer Ellsworth Brown on pp. 57-60. The same papers reprinted in the same order in *N. E. A. Journ. of Proc. and Addr.*, 1910, on pp. 185-190, 190-195, and 195-198 respectively. There is also a reprint by the University of Chicago Press, 1910. The paper of G. P. Brown is printed "without revision or completion just as he left it" in *School and Home Education*, XXIX, 220-224 (March 1910).

Bruce, William George, editorial on "The Death of Dr. Harris" in *American School Board Journal*, XXXIX, No. 6, p. 8 (Dec., 1909). Portrait of Harris on p. 1.

von Bülow-Wendhausen, Bertha, Freiin, *Greeting to America; Reminiscences and Impressions of my Travels; Kindergarten Suggestions.* Translated by L. E. (New York, 1900).

Butler, Nicholas Murray, "William T. Harris," *Educational Review*, XXXVIII, 534-535 (Dec., 1909). Reprinted in *Jour. of Education*, LXXXII, 596 (Dec. 16, 1915) and Perry, Charles Milton, *The St. Louis Movement in Philosophy*, pp. 67-8.
— *The Changes of a Quarter Century* (Address delivered at the 65th Convocation of the University of the State of New York, Albany, N. Y., Oct. 17, 1929). Abstract in Perry, *op. cit.*, pp. 51-54.

Byrne, Lee, "The Committee on Correlation of Studies," *Junior-Senior High School Clearing House*, VI, 197-201 (Dec., 1931).

Canfield, James H., "William Torrey Harris—Teacher, Philosopher, Friend," *American Monthly Review of Reviews*, XXXIV, 164-166 (August, 1906). With portrait.

Cary, Charles P.,—see under Brown, George Pliny and Winship, Albert E.

Cheney, Ednah Dow, *Reminiscences* (Boston, 1902). See Index s.v. Harris, Wm. T.

Clifton, John Leroy, *Ten Famous American Educators* (Columbus, O., 1933), pp. 188-211: "William Torrey Harris; Teacher, Administrator, Philosopher and Writer."

Cohen, Morris R., in *The Cambridge History of American Literature*, III, (New York, 1921), pp. 236-239.

Coleman, William Macon, "William Torrey Harris, Ph.D., LLD., U.S. Commissioner of Education," *Spare-Time Study,* II, No. 3, pp. 1-2, (March, 1899). With portrait.

Commemorative Biographical Record of Tolland and Windham Counties, Connecticut (Chicago, 1903), "Harris" on pp. 559-560.

Compayré, Gabriel, "La Mort de William T. Harris," *Educateur Moderne,* V, 1-2 (Jan., 1910).

Concord Lectures on Philosophy, with an Historical Sketch and arranged by Raymond L. Bridgman (Cambridge, Mass., 1883). 168 pp.

Cook, Francis E., "William Torrey Harris and the St. Louis Public Schools," *Fifty-sixth Annual Report of the Board of Education of the City of St. Louis, 1909-1910,* pp. 23-51. Appeared also as reprint of 31 pp. *Cf.* the Memorial to Dr. Wm. T. Harris by the Board of Education of the City of St. Louis, Nov. 9, 1909, moved by Mr. Woodward, seconded by Mr. Taussig and printed later in the record of the Board.

Cooper, William John, in "The Office of Education," *Scientific Monthly,* XXXVI, on pp. 125-126 (Feb., 1933). With portrait.

Cubberley, Ellwood P., *Public Education in the United States* (Boston, New York, Chicago, 1919). See Index under Harris, William T. and portrait opposite p. 300.

Curti, Merle E., *Social Ideas of American Educators* (New York, 1935), pp. 310-347: "William T. Harris, the Conservator."

Derby, George, editor of article on W. T. Harris in *The National Cyclopædia of American Biography,* XV, 1-2 (New York, 1916.) With portrait, and supplementing article in Vol. IV, 267-268 (New York, 1897). Reprinted as *In Memoriam. William Torrey Harris* (James T. White & Co., New York, 1915), a 12 page pamphlet with portrait and picture of the Putnam Heights, Conn., monument with text taken from Goethe's tribute to Plato and Daniel 12.

Dewey, John, "Harris, *Psychologic Foundations of Education,*" *Educational Review,* XVI, 1-14 (June, 1898).

Dexter, Edwin Grant, *A History of Education in the United States* (New York, 1914), pp. 167, 202-3, 503.

Dodson, G. R., "An Interpretation of the St. Louis Philosophical Movement," *Jour. of Phil., Psy., and Sci. Meth.,* VI, 337-345 (June 24, 1909).

Eaton, General John, *Grant, Lincoln, and the Freedmen* (New York, 1907).

Educational Compendium (Roseburg, Oregon), I, 5 (March, 1890), "William T. Harris, LL.D." From *Educational Courant* of Louisville, Ky., Oct., 1889.

Educational Leadership. Progress and Possibilities. Eleventh Yearbook, published by the Department of Superintendence of the N. E. A. (Feb., 1933). Portrait with biographical note.

Eisler, Rudolf, *Philosophen-Lexikon* (Berlin, 1912), p. 229.

Enciclopedia Universal Ilustrada, article "*Harris—Guillermo Torrey,*" XXVII, (Barcelona, 1925), 753.

Evans, Henry Ridgely, "A List of the Writings of William Torrey Harris, chronologically arranged, with Subject Index," *U. S. Bureau of Education. Report of the Commissioner of Education for 1907,* I, 38-72. "Bibliographical Note" on pp. 37-8. Reprinted and "corrected by" the author in Perry, *The St. Louis Movement in Philosophy,* pp. 96-148.

—   "The Philosophy of William Torrey Harris," *New Age Magazine,* XXVII, 374-378 (Aug., 1919). Recast and reprinted with two portraits under the title of "William Torrey Harris, U. S. Commissioner of Education, 1889 to 1906," *School Life,* XV, 144-147 (April, 1930).

Fitzpatrick, Frank A., "William Torrey Harris: An Appreciation," *Educational Review*, XXXIX, 1-12 (Jan., 1910). Reprinted in *Jour. of Education*, LXXI, 257-9, 312-3, and 340-1 (March, 1910). *Cf.* also LXX, 607 (Dec. 9, 1909).
— —see under Winship, Albert E.

Forbes, Cleon, "The St. Louis School of Thought," Part II, Chapter III, "William Torrey Harris—Exponent," *Missouri Historical Review*, XXV, 289-305 (Jan., 1931). With portrait.

Ford, Thomas Benjamin, "William Torrey Harris, an Educational Reformer." *Internationale Zeitschrift für Erziehung*, IV, 242-250 (Sept. 10, 1935).

Garnett, Christopher Browne, Jr., "The Conception of Individuality in the Philosophy of William Torrey Harris," *Internationale Zeitschrift für Erziehung*, IV, 260-266 (Sept. 10, 1935).

Glenn, G. R.,—see under Winship, Albert E.

Greenwood, James Mickleborough, on Wm. T. Harris in "Some Educators I have Known," *Educational Review*, XXV, 294-7 (March, 1903).
— "U. S. Commissioner W. T. Harris," *School Journal*, LXVIII, 351-2 March 26, 1904).
— "William Torrey Harris—Educator, Philosopher, and Scholar," *Missouri State Teachers' Association. Proceedings and Addresses. 1909*. (Fulton, Mo., 1910), pp. 39-53. Paper read Dec. 28, 1909. Reprinted separately and in *Educational Review*, XXXIX, 121-143 (Feb., 1910). *Cf.* also *Jour. of Education*, LXX, 607 (Dec. 9, 1909).
— "William Torrey Harris," *National Education Association: Journal of Proceedings and Addresses, 1910*, pp. 92-99. A paper read July 5, 1910. Reprinted without major changes under the title of "William Torrey Harris—The Man," *Educational Review*, XL, 173-183 (Sept., 1910).
— see under Winship, Albert E.

Ham, Mrs. Thomas H., *A Genealogy of the Descendants of Nicholas Harris, M. D.* (1904), p. 4.

Harris, David H., *The Early St. Louis Movement* (Los Angeles, 1922). With portrait and other illustrations.

Harris, William Torrey, "How I was Educated," *Forum*, I, 552-561 (Aug., 1886). Reprinted in the *"How I was Educated"* papers (New York, 1888), pp. 50-59.
— "Books That Have Helped Me," *Forum*, III, 142-151 (April, 1887). Reprinted in *"Books That Have Helped Me"* (New York, 1889), pp. 15-34.

Harris, Wm. T., Honors Paid to him on his Retirement from the Superintendency of the St. Louis Public Schools. Contains tributes and editorial of the *St. Louis Globe-Democrat* of June 27, 1880, pp. 1-8; tributes of the *Missouri Republican* and the *St. Louis Times*, pp. 9-11 and 12-15 (both same date); testimonial of the Teachers of the Public Schools, pp. 15-17; article in the *St. Louis Times* for July 4, 1880, describing formal presentation of the resolutions passed by the School Board, pp. 18-24; and extract from the *Am. Jour. of Education* for July, 1880, on pp. 24-25; the State Teachers' Association Resolution of July 25, 1880, pp. 25-26; and a letter of John D. Philbrick to W. T. Harris, notifying him of the appointment by the French Government as Officer of the Academy, on p. 26.

Hogg, Alexander, "Dr. William Torrey Harris," *Jour. of Education*, LXXI, 11 (Jan. 6, 1910).

Holden, Edward S., "William Torrey Harris," *New York Sun*, LXXVII, 8 (Nov. 17, 1909).

Home and School, II, No. 1 (Louisville, Ky., Sept. 20, 1890), "Commissioner Harris." With portrait.

Home, School and Nation, I, 87-8 (Feb., 1890), "Hon. William T. Harris, LL.D." With portrait.

Howard, Jerome B., "William Torrey Harris," *Phonographic Magazine,* XXIII, 296 (Nov., 1909).

Howard, R. H., and Crocker, Henry E., *History of New England* (Boston, 1881). Reference to W. T. Harris in Appendix, p. 12.

Hughes, James L., "World Leaders I Have Known." Subtitle: "William T. Harris, World Leader in Educational Philosophy," *Canadian Magazine,* LXII, 422-424 (Apr., 1924).

Independent, LXI, 469-470 (Aug. 23, 1906), editorial on "The Resignation of Dr. Harris."

International Kindergarten Union, Committee of Nineteen, resolution in regard to Dr. William T. Harris' service to the American Kindergarten in *Kindergarten Review,* XX, 647 (June, 1910).

Internationale Zeitschrift für Erziehung, Studies in Honor of William Torrey Harris on the Occasion of the 100th Return of his Birthday, September 10th, 1935, published with the co-operation of Scholars in America and Abroad. With portrait and dedication. For the articles see under Ford, Garnett, Leidecker, Perry, Roberts, Schwienher, Tufts, Wheelock, Wruck. Summary of all articles, in German, English, and French, pp. 293-296; reprinted in *Hochschule und Ausland,* XIII, No. 10, 85-87 (Oct., 1935).

James, William, in letters to Josiah Royce, *The Letters of William James,* ed. by Henry James (Boston, 1926), pp. 202-204; *cf.* pp. 201-202.
— see under Perry, Ralph Barton.

Johnston, Elizabeth Bryant, "Education in the National Capital. V. Washington History Series," *Home Magazine,* X, Nos. 6, pp. 1, 3, and 16 (June, 1898). With portrait.

Johnson, T. M., "Dr. William T. Harris," *Missouri State Teachers' Association: Proceedings and Addresses.* 1909 (Fulton, Mo., 1910), pp. 53-54.

Kandel, I. L., *Twenty-five Years of American Education* (New York, 1924), pp. 61-63, "Hegelianism."

Karr, Grant, *Dr. W. T. Harris' Lehre von den Grundlagen des Lehrplans Dargestellt und Beurteilt.* Inaugural Dissertation der philosophischen Fakultaet der Universitaet Jena zur Erlangung der Doktorwuerde (Jena, 1900). v, 118 pp.

Kasson, Frank H., "William Torrey Harris, LL.D. His Intellectual Growth and his Educational and Philosophic Work," *Education,* VIII, 619-630 (June, 1888).
— editorial on Harris and his methods as Commissioner of Education, *Education,* XIX, 377-8 (Feb., 1899).
— "William T. Harris," *The* (Boston) *Morning Star,* Oct. 4, 1888.

Kies, Marietta, *Introduction to the Study of Philosophy by William T. Harris.* Comprising passages from his writings selected and arranged with commentary and illustration (New York, 1889); Preface, pp. v-vii.

Lang, Ossian H., "The Commissionership of Education," *Nation,* LXXXIII, No. 2140, pp. 8-9 (July 5, 1906).
— "William T. Harris. An Appreciation," *School Journal,* LXXIII, 31-2 (July 14, 1906).
— "The Educational Outlook," *Forum,* XXXVIII, 217-225 (Oct., 1906).
— "William Torrey Harris," *School Journal,* LXXVII, 125-6 (Dec., 1909).
— "William Torrey Harris, 1835-1909," *National Republic* (Jan., 1936).
— "William T. Harris," *The* (Boston) *Morning Star,* Oct. 4, 1888.

Lathrop, G. P., "Philosophy and Apples," *Atlantic Monthly,* XLVI, 652-6 (Nov., 1880).

Leidecker, Kurt F., "William Torrey Harris und die Deutschen," *New York Staatszeitung und Herold,* Sept. 8, 1935, p. 3, sect. C.
— "William Torrey Harris' Theory of Culture and Civilization," *Internationale Zeitschrift für Erziehung,* IV, 266-278 (Sept. 10, 1935).
— "Harris, ein Kenner Deutschen Geisteslebens," *Troy Freie Presse,* LXV, No. 37, p. 4 (Sept. 14, 1935).
— "William Torrey Harris, 1835-1909," *National Republic* (Jan., 1936).

Lefevre, Arthur, on the Commissionership of W. T. Harris, *Texas School Journal,* XXIV, No. 1, 17-18 (Sept., 1906).

Lincoln Library of Essential Information (Frontier Press Co., 1929), p. 1633.

Literary World, XIV, 272 (August 25, 1883), "Philosophy at Concord."

Mark, H. Thiselton, *Individuality and the Moral Aim of American Education* (London, 1901), 298 pp. This book is dedicated to "The Hon. William Torrey Harris, Ph.D., LL.D., Commissioner of Education of the United States of America, with the writer's high esteem and profound gratitude for help unstintingly given and in grateful remembrance of many words and deeds of welcome from American educators," and Harris is frequently quoted throughout.

McConnell, Robert E., "The Leadership Qualities of William T. Harris," *Kadelpian Review,* IX, 209-216 (March, 1930).

McCosh, James, "The Concord School of Philosophy," *Princeton Review,* n.s. IX, 49-71 (January, 1882).

McGilvary, E. B., "Dr. William T. Harris," *University of California Magazine,* III, 24-31 (Feb., 1897).

Massachusetts Schoolmasters' Club, *In Memoriam William Torrey Harris, LL.D. 1835-1909.* 4 pp.

Mathewson, Arthur, "Our Most Honored Alumnus," *Woodstock Academy Gleaner,* III, No. 2, pp. 4-5 (Aug., 1906).

Mead, Edwin D., "William Torrey Harris," *Boston Evening Transcript,* LXXX, 12 (Nov. 9, 1909). Reprinted in *Bulletin of the Brooklyn Institute of Arts and Sciences,* III, 338 and 343 (Dec. 4, 1909), with full-page portrait.

Mead, Lucia Ames, "William Torrey Harris's Philosophy," *Jour. of Education,* CI, 696-7 (June 18, 1925).
— —see under Winship, Albert E.

de Menil, Alexander N., *The Literature of the Louisiana Territory* (St. Louis, 1904), pp. 191-6.

Mirror, St. Louis, Mo., Nov. 11, 1909. Obituary notice.

Misawa, Tadasu, "William Torrey Harris," *Modern Educators and their Ideals* (New York, 1909), pp. 267-276.

Monroe, Will Seymour, *The Educational Labors of William T. Harris* (Syracuse, N. Y., 1897).
— *Pestalozzian Movement in the United States* (Syracuse, N. Y., 1907), Ch. IX on "William T. Harris and Pestalozzianism in the Schools of St. Louis," pp. 195-203. With portrait.

Morant, Sir Robert L., "The National Bureau of Education in the United States," *Special Reports on Educational Subjects, 1896-7* (London 1897), pp. 647-657. Reprinted under later date.

Morgan, H. H., "Account of the St. Louis Movement," *History of St. Louis, City and County,* ed. J. T. Scharf (Philadelphia, 1899), II, 1599-1612.

Mowry, William Augustus, *Recollections of a New England Educator* (New York, 1908). See Index.
— "William T. Harris, LL. D.; his Early Life and his St. Louis Reports," *American Education,* XIII, 308-311 (March, 1910).
— "Reminiscences of Dr. Harris," *Jour. of Education,* LXX, 629-630 (Dec. 16, 1909).
— "William T. Harris," *Jour. of Education,* LXXXIII, 90-91 (Jan. 27, 1916).
— "William T. Harris and the Bureau of Education," *New England Magazine,* n.s. I, 183-6 (Oct., 1889). With portrait.

Muirhead, John H., "How Hegel Came to America," *Phil. Review,* XXXVII, 226-240 (May, 1928).
— *The Platonic Tradition in Anglo-Saxon Philosophy* (New York, 1931), pp. 319-323. Cf. Index.

Nation, XXXI, 74 (July 29, 1880), "Philosophy at Concord." LVII, 103-4 (Aug. 10, 1893), review of F. B. Sanborn and W. T. Harris' *A. Bronson Alcott: His Life and Philosophy.* Cf. Sanborn's reply, p. 136 (Aug. 24), and *Critic,* XXII, 348-9 (May 27, 1893), with picture of Alcott and Harris in front of the Old Orchard House.

National Educator (Allentown, Penna.), XXX, No. 9, p. 1 (Aug. 15, 1889), "William Torrey Harris."

New England Magazine, n.s. XXVIII, 538 (July, 1903). With portrait.

New York Education, II, 405-6 (March, 1899), "Dr. William T. Harris." Portrait on front cover.

New York Evening Post, Nov. 6, 1909. Obituary notice.

Niel, Harriet, "William Torrey Harris," *Pioneers of the Kindergarten in America* (Century Co., New York and London, 1924), pp. 167-183.

Normal News, XV, No. 2, 8-9 (Oct. 1895), "William Torrey Harris." With portrait.

Outlook, LXXX, 735-6 (July 22, 1905), in "Public School Leaders." With portrait.
— XCIII, 611-2 (Nov. 20, 1909), "A Thinker in Education."

Pallen, Condé B., "The Concord School of Philosophy," *American Catholic Quarterly Review,* XIII, 555-565 (July, 1888).

Palmer, Frank H., editorial on the passing away of W. T. Harris, *Education,* XXX, 247 (Dec., 1909). See above under Boone.

Pennsylvania School Journal, LVIII, 281-2 (Dec., 1909). Obituary notice.

Perry, Charles Milton, *The St. Louis Movement in Philosophy. Some Source Material* (Norman, Okla., 1930). 148 pp. Contains letters speaking of Harris, bibliographical material and Evans' corrected list of Harris' writings.
— "Unknown Quantities in the St. Louis Movement," *Internationale Zeitschrift für Erziehung,* IV, 278-284 (Sept. 10, 1935).

Perry, Ralph Barton, *The Thought and Character of William James* (Boston, 1935), I, 465, 712, 726, 732, 736, 740, 742, 749, 753, 781, 786; II, 160, 288.

Phrenological Journal XCII, 102-3 (Sept., 1891), "William T. Harris." Portrait on p. 101.

Pierce, Lovick, Sketch of Dr. William T. Harris, United States Commissioner of Education, in *Georgia Education,* I, 7 (July 15, 1899).

Popular Science Monthly, LXIX, 283-5 (Sept., 1906) : "The Bureau of Education." With portrait.

Providence (R. I.) *Daily Journal,* Nov. 6, 1909: obituary notice with brief biography.
— Nov. 10, 1909: report of funeral of W. T. Harris with quotations from orations of Elmer Ellsworth Brown and F. B. Sanborn.

Quick, Robert Herbert, *Essays on Educational Reformers* (New York, 1898), Index. *Cf. Life and Remains of the Rev. R. H. Quick,* ed. F. Storr (New York, 1899), pp. 512-514.

Raup, R. B., "Harris, William Torrey," *Encyclopaedia of the Social Sciences,* VII (New York, 1932), p. 274.

Richardson, Charles F., *American Literature* (New York, 1898), I, 322-5.

Riley, Woodbridge, *American Thought from Puritanism to Pragmatism* (New York, 1915), pp. 240-253: "The St. Louis School: William T. Harris."

Roberts, John Stacey, *William T. Harris. A Critical Study of his Educational and Related Philosophical Views.* (Washington, D. C., 1924). xvi, 250 pp.
— "Educational Contributions of William Torrey Harris," *Internationale Zeitschrift für Erziehung,* IV, 237-242 (Sept. 10, 1935).

Sabin, Henry, "Reminiscenses of William Torrey Harris," *Jour. of Education,* LXXI, 483-4 (May 5, 1910).

Sadler, Michael E., "Influence of the late Dr. W. T. Harris in English Education," *Jour. of Education* (London) n.s. XXXII, 78 and 80 (Jan., 1910).
— "The Service of William Torrey Harris to British Education," *Educational Review,* XXXIX, 191-4 (Feb., 1910).

St. Louis Globe-Democrat, Aug. 8, 1922: "Tribute Paid to William Torrey Harris, LL.D." Reprinted for private circulation. *Cf.* also this paper for Feb. 27, 1933: "William T. Harris Honored as Leader by Educators Body"; Apr. 28, 1935: "Philosophers of U. S. to Honor Renowned Dr. William T. Harris"; May 3, 1935: "Prof. W. T. Harris Memorialized as Philosophers Meet." See also under *Harris, Wm. T. Honors Paid to him.*

St. Louis Post-Dispatch, May 3, 1935: "Philosophers' Tribute to William T. Harris."

Sanborn, F. B., *Recollections of Seventy Years* (Boston, 1909), II, 485-513: "The Concord School of Philosophy." Portraits.
— "William T. Harris," *Springfield* (Mass.) *Republican,* Nov. 11 and 13, 1909. Reprinted in *Boston Transcript,* Nov. 15, 1909.
— —see under *Providence* (R. I.) *Daily Journal.*

Sandison, Howard, "A Study of Dr. Harris' Foundations of Education," *Inland Educator and Inland School Journal* (Indianapolis, Ind.), beginning with vol. II, No. 1 (Sept., 1901) and carried through the following years.

School Century, V, 153-4 (Dec., 1909) : obituary notice.

School Journal, LXX, 300 (March 18, 1905) : editorial on "The Bureau of Education."

Schuyler, William, "German Philosophy in St. Louis," *Bulletin of the Washington University Association* (St. Louis, 1904), pp. 62-84. "Reprinted, with slight changes" as "The St. Louis Philosophical Movement," *Educational Review,* XXIX, 450-467 (May, 1905).

Schwienher, Lucy M., "William T. Harris," *Educational Administration and Supervision,* including *Teacher Training,* XIX, 227-231 (March, 1933).
— "William Torrey Harris, Influence of his St. Louis Period," *Internationale Zeitschrift für Erziehung,* IV, 254-260 (Sept. 10, 1935).

Sewall, Frank, review of W. T. Harris' *The Spiritual Sense of Dante's Divina Commedia* in *New Jerusalem Magazine,* XV, No. 9 (Sept., 1891). The same in *Dante and Swedenborg* (London, 1893), pp. 60-80.

Smith, Anna Tolman, "The National Bureau of Education and Dr. W. T. Harris," *Home Magazine,* Feb., 1890, p. 10. With portrait.
— "Expansion of the Bureau of Education," *Educational Review,* XLIII, 310-3 (March, 1912).
— —see under Winship, Albert E.

Smith, Darrell Hevenor, *The Bureau of Education* (Baltimore, 1923), pp. 13-15.

Snider, Denton J., *A Writer of Books in his Genesis* (St. Louis, 1910), in chapter "At St. Louis" and elsewhere references to W. T. Harris.
— *The St. Louis Movement in Philosophy, Literature, Education, Psychology, with Chapters of Autobiography* (St. Louis, 1920).

Snyder, Rev. John, "The Higher Life of St. Louis," *Outlook,* LIV; Harris mentioned on p. 373 and portrait on p. 376 (Aug. 29, 1896).

Springfield (Mass.) *Republican,* obituary notice, Nov. 6, 1909; editorial, Nov. 7, 1909.—See also under Sanborn, F. B.

Stevens, M. *"The National Bureau of Education,"* School Journal, LVI, 743-750 (June 25, 1898). With portrait.

Stokes, Anson Phelps, "William Torrey Harris," *Memorials of Eminent Yale Men* (New Haven, 1914), I, 273-280.

Story of Concord Told by Concord Writers, ed. Josephine Latham Swayne (Boston, 1906). See Index s.v. Harris, William T.

Strawn, Arthur, "A Short View of St. Louis," *American Mercury,* X, 470-477 (April, 1927).

Sutton, William Seneca, "Contributions of William Torrey Harris to the Development of Education in America," *Educational Review,* XXXIX, 299-308 (March, 1910). A paper read at a memorial service held in honor of Harris by the Students' Association of the Department of Education of the University of Texas, Jan. 25, 1910. Reprinted in Sutton, *Problems in Modern Education* (Boston, 1913), pp. 140-153.
— article on W. T. Harris in *A Cyclopedia of Education,* ed. Paul Monroe, III, (New York, 1912), pp. 219-220. With portrait. Quotation from this article in *American School Board Journal,* LXXXII, 40 (March, 1931), accompanied by portrait.

Thwing, Charles Franklin, *A History of Education in the United States since the Civil War* (Boston and New York, 1910), pp. 309-313.
— "Happy Yesterdays of a University President. VIII: William Torrey Harris," *Congregationalist,* CVII, 618-9 (May 18, 1922).
— *Guides, Philosophers and Friends. Studies of College Men* (New York, 1927), Ch. VII: "William Torrey Harris. The Metaphysician who was also an Educational Administrator," pp. 144-159.

Tigert, John James, "An Appreciation of William Torrey Harris, Educator and Philosopher," *National Education Association. Proceedings 1927,* pp. 179-184. An address printed in abridged form. *Cf.* his "Address of Welcome," *Jour. of Education,* C, 101-2 (July 24, 1924).

Torrey, Frederic C., *The Torrey Families and their Children in America* (Lakehurst, N. J., 1924), I, 214-6. With portrait.

Townsend, Harvey Gates, *Philosophical Ideas in the United States* (New York, 1934), pp. 116-130.

Treudly, T. (Misprint for Frederick), "Dr. William T. Harris," *Education*, XXXI, 231-7 (Dec., 1910).

Tufts, James Hayden, editorial on the death of W. T. Harris in *School Review*, XVII, 717 (Dec., 1909).
— "William Torrey Harris—A Personal Impression," *Internationale Zeitschrift für Erziehung*, IV, 235-6 (Sept. 10, 1935).

Twentieth Century Biographical Dictionary of Notable Americans, Rossiter Johnson, ed., V (Boston, 1904), s.v. Harris, William Torrey.

Ueberweg, Friedrich, *Grundriss der Geschichte der Philosophie*. V. Teil; *Die Philosophie des Auslandes vom Beginn des 19ten Jahrhunderts bis auf die Gegenwart* (12. Aufl., herausg. von Dr. T. K. Oesterreich. Berlin, 1928), pp. 379-380.

Underwood, Mr. and Mrs. B. F., editorial on "The Concord School of Philosophy," *Open Court*, I, 355-357 (Aug. 4, 1887).

Vail, Walter Scott, "Hon. William T. Harris," *St. Paul Dispatch*, July 9, 1890.

Vandewalker, Nina C., *The Kindergarten in American Education* (New York, 1908). See Index.

Ward, Julius H. "The Concord School of Philosophy," *International Review*, IX, 459-467 (Oct., 1880).

Wheelock, Lucy, "William Torrey Harris and the Kindergarten," *Internationale Zeitschrift für Erziehung*, IV, 251-3 (Sept. 10, 1935).

Whiting, Lilian, "A Group of St. Louis Idealists," *Theosophical Path*, VII, 356-362 (Nov., 1914). With portrait.
— *The Golden Road* (Boston, 1918). Occasional references to W. T. Harris.

Who's Who in America, 1908-9, p. 828, "Harris, William Torrey."

Winship, Albert E., "William Torrey Harris," in *Jour. of Education* XLIV, 264-265 (Oct. 15, 1896).
— "The Retirement of Dr. W. T. Harris" in *Jour. of Education*, LXIII. 18 (June 28, 1906).
— "A Harris Monument," *Jour of Education*, LXXI, 240 (March 3, 1910).
— "The Appointment of Dr. Harris," *Jour. of Education*, LXXI, 369-370 (Apr. 7, 1910).
— "In Remembrance of William T. Harris," *Jour. of Education*, LXXXII, 593-6. *Cf.* p. 604 (Dec. 16, 1915). With portrait. This article by the editor is the first of a symposium (pp. 593-603 and 607-8), the rest being by Nicholas Murray Butler, John W. Cook, Elmer Ellsworth Brown, G. R. Glenn, Henry Sabin, Nathan C. Schaeffer, Joseph Swain, Lucia Ames Mead, Mrs. Frank A. Fitzpatrick, Mrs. J. M. Greenwood, John Mac-Donald, Anna Tolman Smith, C. P. Cary, Albert Leonard, A. R. Taylor, Carroll G. Pearse, Walter E. Ranger, Charles M. Jordan, Guy Potter Benton, D. B. Johnson, Ben Blewett, J. W. Crabtree, Homer H. Seerley, M. P. Shawkey, Calvin N. Kendall, Mason S. Stone, J. M. Green, A. G. Baker, William McAndrew, Robert J. Aley, O. T. Corson, Charles R. Skinner, Franklin B. Dyer, L. C. Lord, John D. Shoop,

I. I. Cammack. *Cf.* also the "Tributes to William Torrey Harris" which Winship printed with portrait, *ibid.*, LXX, 607-8 and 610 (Dec. 9, 1909), including tributes by J. M. Greenwood, Frank A. Fitzpatrick, William Estabrook Chancellor, Ben Blewett and C. H. Ames.

— "Educators as I have known them." Subtitle: "United States Commissioners of Education—(IV). William Torrey Harris," *Jour. of Education*, LXXXIII, 541-2 (May 18, 1916). *Cf.* his editorial: "Dr. W. T. Harris: Ex-U. S. Commissioner of Education," LXX, 464-5 (Nov. 4, 1909) and his editorial: "The Death of Dr. Harris" on p. 490 (Nov. 11, 1909).

— "Pioneers in Education—(X). Dr. William T. Harris," *Jour. of Education*, XCVIII, 481 (Nov. 28, 1923).

— "Friends and Acquaintances (IV). William Torrey Harris," *Jour. of Education*, CI, 603-7 (May 28, 1925).

— on the portrait of William T. Harris in the Bureau of Education, *Jour. of Education*, LIII, 288 (March 18, 1926).

Woerner, J. Gabriel, *The Rebel's Daughter* (Boston, 1899). Harris figures in this novel as "Professor Altrue." *Cf.* Perry, *The St. Louis Movement in Philosophy*, pp. 41-2, 44 for further reference.

Wruck, Johannes, "Harris und die deutsche Philosophie," *Internationale Zeitschrift für Erziehung*, IV, 285-292 (Sept. 10, 1935).

Yale Alumni Weekly, XIX, 193 (Nov. 12, 1909). Obituary notice.

Yale University, *Obituary Record of Yale Graduates*, 1909-1910, pp. 1198-1201.

Young, Mrs. Ella (Flagg), in *National Education Association. Journal of Proceedings and Addresses, 1907*, pp. 384-6. This part dealing with Harris and including correspondence of Henry S. Pritchett and Theodore Roosevelt reprinted in *Jour. of Education*, LXVI, 255-7 (Sept. 12, 1907) under the title of "Dr. William T. Harris. A Notable Tribute."